CHINA TOWNS

ASIAN
COOKING
FROM AROUND
THE WORLD IN
100 RECIPES

CHINA TOWNS

Text: Emmanuelle Jary
Design: Marie-Paule Jaulme

JEAN-FRANÇOIS MALLET

jacqui small

INTRODUCTION

'Tonight we're eating Chinese'! In the restaurant, we're seated in front of nems, a beef and citronella salad, a roasted Peking duck and fried rice. But these various dishes have in fact travelled thousands of kilometres and crossed several borders. The equivalent of this meal in Europe would be an Andalusian gazpacho, a beef bourguignon, a slice of Neapolitan pizza and a few Swedish pickled herring. The nem is Vietnamese, the beef and citronella salad is Thai, the roasted duck is from Peking and the Cantonese rice, as the name suggests, comes from South China, more than 2,000 km (1,240 miles) away from the capital. This is the way we have eaten 'Chinese' in the West for a long time, but for several years, however, restaurants in large cities, and particularly in capitals such as Paris, London, Canberra and Washington D.C., have been specializing in just one cuisine. Some serve only Vietnamese food, others Thai dishes, and others Cambodian, Lao or simply Chinese, namely Cantonese, cuisine, but here again, 'Chinese' does not really mean anything.

Four broad culinary families distinguish themselves in China, which is fourteen times larger than France. The cuisine of Northeastern China (Shandong and Beijing) is rich and powerful, and grants a special place to lamb, which is rare in other parts of the country. The Southeastern cuisine (Jiangsu, Anhui, Zhejiang) is composed of many vegetables and freshwater fish, while the food of South China (Fujian, Guangdong), the famous Cantonese cuisine, is the most widespread throughout the world. It favours steam-cooking, which retains the freshness of the ingredients used, some of which Westerners find off-putting, for example dog, snake, mouse and cat. Finally, the cuisine of Southwestern China (Hunan and Sichuan) is extremely hot. Sichuan pepper is well known in the West, however, it is not actually a pepper, but rather a berry that creates a strange numbing sensation in the mouth. Asian cuisine, and in particular Chinese, is not focused exclusively on flavours: temperature and textures – hot, cold, crispy, sticky, cartilaginous, soft, hard, liquid, runny, spicy, bitter, sweet-and-sour, salty, sweet, sour and even bland – are also essential. The mouth is the focus of many sensations, all of them delightful.

Why do we in the West use 'Chinese' to talk about Asian cuisine as a whole? Probably because the first big wave of immigration from Asia was Chinese. The Chinese presence in Europe goes back 700 years, when 140,000 workers from Wenzhou, a town on the East coast of China, flocked to England and France to work in factories and dig trenches during the First World War. After the war, some opened restaurants in Paris next to the Gare de Lyon and others migrated to

Marseille. From the 1930s to the 1950s, this population moved around the 3rd arrondissement, towards the rue au Maire and the rue Volta, where many Chinese still reside, working in leatherwear, the textile industry and selling costume jewellery. Authentic Chinese restaurants from Wenzhou are also found in this neighbourhood. The town, extremely poor in the past, is today one of the wealthiest in China, notably thanks to money coming from families living abroad.

From the 1960s to the 1970s, the second big wave of immigration (about 40,000 people) was made up of political refugees who had arrived as boat people and were fleeing from the Vietnam War or the Pol Pot regime in Cambodia. First came the Chinese from Indochina, who were followed by Vietnamese and Cambodians. They settled in Paris's 13th arrondissement, where the famous Olympiades tower blocks had just been erected, a huge Parisian real estate project that hadn't met with as much success and enthusiasm from the French as had been hoped. In the 1980s and 1990s, the Choisi triangle (the avenue d'Ivry, the avenue de Choisy, the boulevard Massena and the Olympiades towers) was full of these political refugees, so the new immigrants from China went to live in the suburbs, in particular in Logne and Marne-la-Vallée in Seine-et-Marne. However, they continue to work in Paris (restaurants and small businesses) and have set up in the north of the city around Belleville.

During the same period, the United States also experienced high levels of immigration from both China (Shanghai, Fujian, Guangzhou) and Vietnam, at the time of the Vietnam War. The world's largest Chinatown is located in San Francisco where the architecture is more typically Chinese than in Paris. In New York, Chinatown is located in the south of Manhattan. The culture shock is instant: fish swimming in tanks, swallows' nests, shark fins, canned sea cucumber, etc. For Chinese New Year, parades and dragon dances are organized in the streets. The largest wave of immigration to the United Kingdom during the 1950s was from Hong Kong, where unemployed Chinese farmers decided that it was more profitable to lease their land and go and settle in Britain, mainly in the Greater London Area.

No matter where they settle, Japanese immigrants have tended not to mix with Chinese and Asians from the old Indochinese peninsula. (In Paris, a Japanese neighbourhood is located to the north of the Palais Royal.) The same applies to Koreans, whose restaurants are found all over Paris, while Thai restaurants are found in various Chinatowns although they are not necessarily run by Thai.

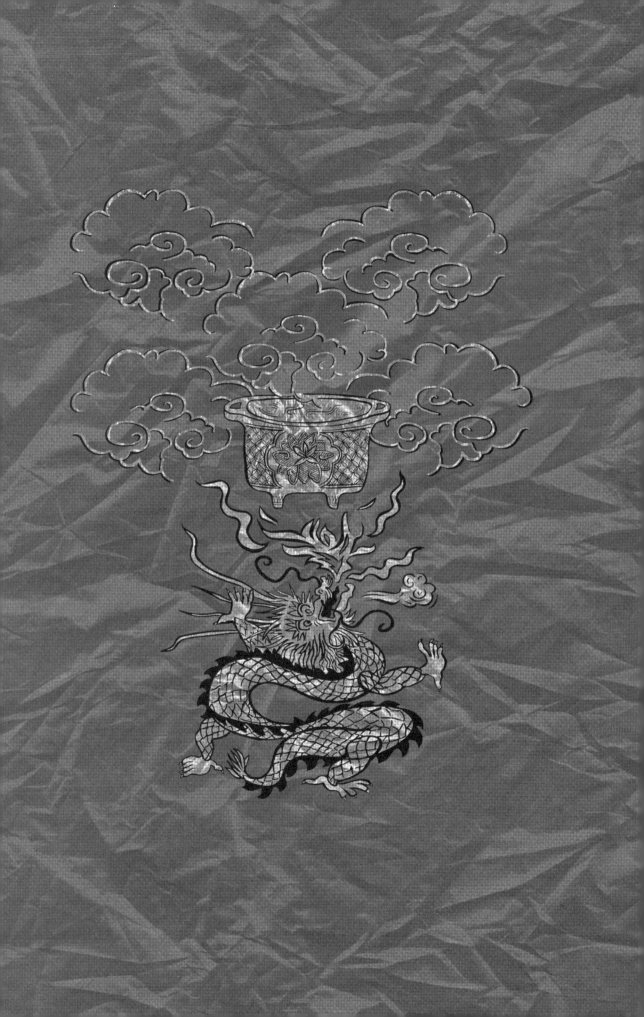

CONTENTS

STARTERS *PAGE 10*

CHINESE DUMPLINGS *PAGE 36*

SOUPS & BROTHS *PAGE 62*

CHICKEN & QUAIL *PAGE 102*

BEEF *PAGE 134*

PORK *PAGE 166*

DUCK *PAGE 200*

FISH & SEAFOOD *PAGE 242*

WEIRD & WONDERFUL *PAGE 280*

VEGETABLE, RICE & SIDE DISHES *PAGE 318*

NOODLES *PAGE 354*

TEA, DRINKS & DESSERTS *PAGE 378*

Recipe Index *PAGE 412*

Chinatowns Around the World *PAGE 414*

Acknowledgements *PAGE 415*

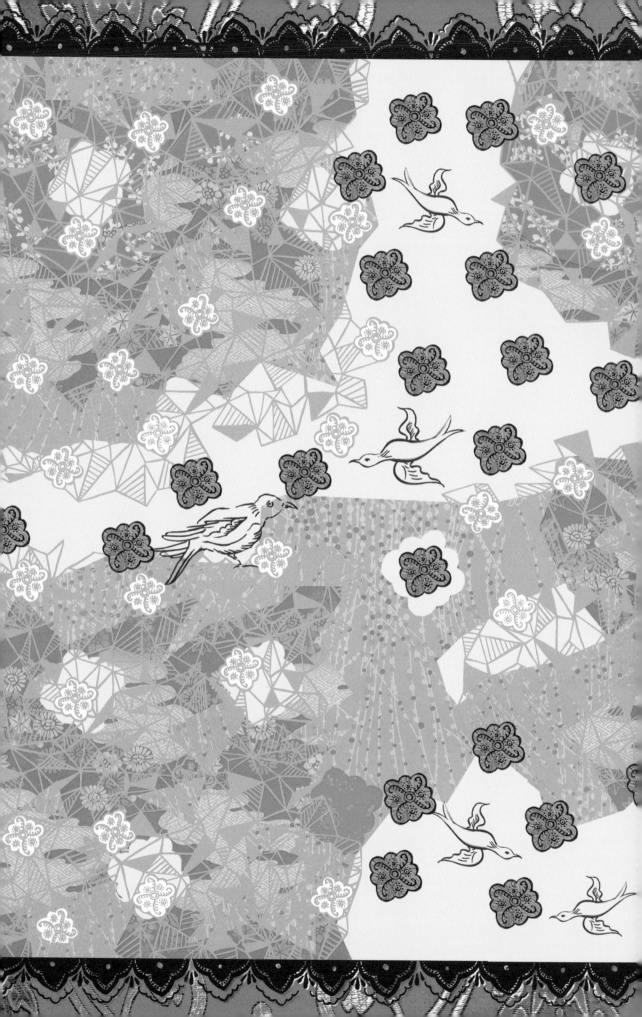

STARTERS

STARTERS

Meals in Southeast Asia, as in China, do not follow a set format of starter, main and dessert as they do in the West. The dishes are all served at the same time and shared by the whole table, so guests can help themselves according to their own taste and appetite. The term 'starter' doesn't really mean anything in Asia, nevertheless, Asian restaurants in the West have adapted to suit the traditional eating habits of their customers. Menus are divided into starters, meat dishes, fish dishes and desserts, so soups, salads and other smaller dishes are found under starters. In the West dish of kebabs, dumplings, soup or salad would be eaten at the beginning of a meal.

Menus typically have a selection of salads: with lemongrass and lots of fresh herbs in a Thai restaurant; with chicken or seafood in a Chinese restaurant. In Vietnamese restaurants, nems are often cut up and served in pieces in main meals such as *bo bun*. Nems are Vietnamese, but you can find various types of fried roll or *spring roll* throughout Asia, in particular in China and Thailand. They are prepared with wraps made from wheat flour rather than rice flour and are usually filled with cabbage, carrots and mushrooms. The fillings can be vegetarian or meat. In Vietnam, spring rolls are served mainly raw and rolled in a rice sheet filled with bean sprouts, vermicelli, lettuce, fresh mint and either prawns (shrimp) or beef. Chinese or Vietnamese dumplings are also often listed under starters.

Even so, it is quite nice to eat a salad at the same time as a meat or fish dish and plain rice, or to take a bite of a dumpling in between two spoonfuls of soup. In other words to eat as the Asians do when in a Chinese, Vietnamese or Cambodian restaurant, but it's never too late to change our traditional habits! Chinese restaurants in the West often list this kind of dish under starters.

Salted hard-boiled eggs
(served for breakfast)
and lacy pork dumplings

Spring rolls with crab and pork (p26)

Sticky rice in banana leaves

Preparing nems for cooking

'Mo', small buns cooked on a hot plate,
traditionally filled with pork, but made here
with fried duck's liver

'GOI CUON' SPRING ROLLS

SERVES 4

Preparation: 45 min

8 lettuce leaves

30g (1oz) rice vermicelli

20 mint leaves

10 Thai basil leaves

8 large cooked prawns
(shrimp)

3 fresh garlic stems

4 large rice paper wraps

For the sauce:

2 limes

1 garlic clove

2 tbsp caster (superfine) sugar

6 tbsp nuoc-mâm

6 tbsp water

2 tbsp hoisin sauce

1 tsp chilli paste

2 tbsp roasted peanuts

Rinse and dry the lettuce, cut out the tough parts and roughly chop the leaves. Drop the vermicelli into boiling water for 3 minutes, drain and rinse under cold water and chop finely. Rinse and roughly chop the mint and basil leaves, then peel and cut the prawns (shrimp) in half lengthways with a sharp knife.

For the sauce, squeeze the limes, then peel and crush the garlic. Mix together the garlic, sugar, nuoc-mâm, water, lime juice, hoisin sauce and chilli paste and set aside.

Cut the garlic stems in half. Dip the rice wrappers, one at a time, into a bowl of hot water for 1 second, or until pliable, then place them on the work surface (counter). Place the halved prawns (shrimp) in the middle, then add the rice vermicelli, the herbs and the lettuce. Fold the sides of the wraps over the filling, add a garlic stem and roll up tightly. Crush the peanuts, add them to the sauce and enjoy.

VIETNAMESE PRAWN SALAD

SERVES 4

Preparation: 25 min

20 cooked prawns (shrimp)
8 lettuce leaves
4 spring onion (scallion) stems
1 bunch of coriander
(cilantro)
½ a cucumber
1 large carrot

3 tbsp roasted peanuts
150g (5½oz/1½ cups)
bean sprouts

For the sauce:
1 garlic clove
2 tbsp water

2 tbsp nuoc-mâm
1 tsp caster (superfine) sugar
¼ tsp chilli paste
juice of 1 lime
2 tbsp groundnut
(peanut) oil

For the sauce, peel and chop the garlic, then mix the water, nuoc-mâm, sugar, chilli paste, lime juice, garlic and oil in a bowl and set aside.

Cut the prawns (shrimp) in half lengthways and set aside. Rinse the lettuce and cut into large pieces, chop the spring onion (scallion), then rinse, dry and roughly chop the coriander (cilantro) with its stalks.

Rinse the cucumber, deseed and cut into thin strips then peel and grate the carrot using a wide grater setting. Use a mortar and pestle to grind the peanuts into rough pieces. Drop the bean sprouts into a pan of boiling water for 2 seconds, then drain.

Mix all the vegetables, the lettuce and herbs with the sauce then arrange in a serving dish. Place the prawns (shrimp) on top, sprinkle over the peanuts and serve straight away.

RECIPE
PAGE
26

SHRIMP AND PORK ROLLS

P. 22 • SERVES 4

Preparation: 1 hr

50g (1¾oz) dried shrimps, 8 lettuce leaves, 20 mint leaves, 20 Thai basil leaves, 1 bunch of coriander (cilantro), ½ a cucumber, 100g (3½oz) crispy pork (available in Asian grocery stores, or the remains of a pork roast), 8 small rice wrappers
For the sauce: 2 limes, 1 garlic clove, 2 tbsp caster (superfine) sugar, 6 tbsp nuoc-mâm, 6 tbsp water

Soak the shrimps in a bowl of warm water for 15 minutes, then drain. Rinse, dry and cut the lettuce leaves in half. Rinse, remove the stalks and roughly chop the mint, basil and coriander (cilantro). Rinse the cucumber and cut into small strips. For the sauce, squeeze the limes. Peel and crush the garlic, then mix the garlic, sugar, nuoc-mâm, water and lime juice together. Chop the pork into thin slices. Plunge the rice wrappers, one at a time, into warm water for 1 second, or until pliable then place on the work surface (counter). Place the pork in the middle. Add the cucumber slices, shrimps, herbs and lettuce, fold the edges of the wrapper over the filling and roll up tightly. Serve with the sauce.

SPRING ROLLS WITH CRAB AND PORK

P. 23 • SERVES 4

Preparation: 30 min • Cooking time: 20 min

1 bunch of coriander (cilantro), 80g (3oz) taro, 1 x 240g (8½oz)can crabmeat, 100g (3½oz) sausage meat, 1 tbsp soy sauce, 1 tsp nuoc mâm, 8 medium rice wrappers, 2 tbsp cornflour (cornstarch), 1 egg, cooking oil

Rinse and chop three quarters of the coriander (cilantro). Steam the taro for 15 minutes until soft then mash. Mix the crab with the sausage meat and taro, add the chopped coriander (cilantro), soy sauce and nuoc-mâm and mix thoroughly. Wet the rice wrappers with a damp cloth. Spread them out two at a time so that they overlap. Place the filling in the middle, fold the edges over the filling then roll up into neat, tight rolls. Prepare and heat a deep-fryer. Sprinkle the rolls with cornflour (cornstarch), then carefully lower them into the hot oil and deep-fry for 5 minutes, shaking regularly. Drain on kitchen paper (paper towels), then cut them into four. Arrange the spring rolls on a large plate, garnish with the remaining coriander (cilantro) and serve with sweet chilli sauce.

SAIGON CRAB NEMS

P. 24 • SERVES 6

Preparation: 45 min • **Cooking time:** 40 min

150g (5½oz) vermicelli, 5 dried black mushrooms, 200g (7oz) good-quality crabmeat, 200g (7oz/2 cups) bean sprouts, 7 spring onion (scallion) stems, 80g (3oz) minced (ground) pork, 1 egg, 2 tbsp nuoc-mâm, 30 small sheets of rice paper, a few lettuce leaves, 1 bunch of mint, 10 Thai basil sprigs, 20 shiso leaves, 1 small cucumber, cooking oil
For the sauce: 30g (1oz) green papaya, peeled and finely grated, 1 small red chilli, finely chopped, 2 garlic cloves, 2 tbsp warm water, 2 tbsp nuoc-mâm, 2 tbsp caster (superfine) sugar, 2 tbsp rice vinegar, juice of 1 lime

Drop the vermicelli into warm water for 20 minutes, then drain and roughly chop. Drop the black mushrooms into warm water for 10 minutes, then drain, trim and chop them into small pieces. Rinse and drain the crabmeat. Drop the bean sprouts into a pan of boiling water for 1 minute then drain and set aside. Rinse and chop the spring onions (scallions). Mix together the crab, pork, vermicelli, egg, mushrooms, nuoc-mâm, bean sprouts and spring onions (scallions). Soften a sheet of rice paper by leaving it for 3–4 minutes between two tea (dish) towels soaked in warm water. Place a little of the filling in the middle, then fold the edges over the filling and roll up tightly. Set the rolls aside as you make them and leave them to dry for 20 minutes at room temperature. Mix all the sauce ingredients together and set aside. Prepare and heat a deep-fryer. Carefully lower the nems, six at a time, into the hot oil and deep-fry for 6–8 minutes. Drain and serve with the sauce, lettuce, herbs and cucumber.

'AMOK'

P. 25 • SERVES 4

Preparation: 30 min • **Cooking time:** 15 min

700g (1lb 9oz) boneless white fish flesh (cod, pollock, hake or anything similar), 1 egg, 30g (1oz) piece ginger, 30g (1oz) piece galangal, 4 lemongrass stalks, 1 garlic clove, 1 onion, 2 tbsp nuoc-mâm, 600ml (20fl oz/2½ cups) coconut milk + 100ml (3½fl oz/scant ½ cup), 1 tsp ground turmeric, 1 tbsp paprika; ½ red (bell) pepper, 5 chive sprigs

Mix the fish with the egg, then peel the ginger and galangal and grate them. Remove the hard outer covering of the lemongrass and slice the rest. Chop the garlic and onion finely, then put the ginger, galangal, lemongrass, garlic and onion in a mortar and grind with a pestle until smooth. Heat the nuoc-mâm, fish, coconut milk, turmeric and paprika togther then add them to the ginger mixture and mix everything together until thick. Form the mixture into small balls, about the size of an egg, and lay them out on a plate. Steam them for about 15 minutes. Garnish with slices of pepper and chives. Add a little emulsified coconut milk (use a blender for this) and serve.

'YAM'
WITH BEEF

SERVES 4–6

Preparation: 35 min • **Cooking time:** 10 min

---

1 large carrot
2 bunches of coriander
(cilantro)
½ a cucumber
1 red chilli

3 lemongrass stalks
1 tsp caster (superfine) sugar
2 tbsp light soy sauce
4 tbsp nuoc mâm
juice of 3 limes

2 sweet onions
500g (1lb 2oz) beef
(rump steak or fillet/tenderloin)
20 mint leaves

Peel and grate the carrot, then rinse, dry and roughly chop the coriander (cilantro) with its stalks. Peel the cucumber, deseed and chop finely, then trim the chilli and chop finely. Remove the hard outer covering of the lemongrass and chop the rest.

Mix the sugar, soy sauce, nuoc-mâm and lime juice together in a bowl. Peel and chop the onions.

Seal the beef in a large hot frying pan without adding any fat and cook each side for 3–4 minutes, according to taste. Leave to stand for 5 minutes. Mix the coriander (cilantro), mint, onions, chilli, lemongrass, carrot and cucumber together in a bowl. Slice the meat into thin pieces, add to the bowl and serve.

SUKHO THAI

Paris

'We are Cambodian Chinese', explain the owners. 'But our restaurant serves Thai food, with a few additional Chinese specialities.' We are talking about one of the best Thai restaurants in Paris. Our advice for the more adventurous is to try the house salad with Thai beans, a quite extraordinary culinary dish: a strange green vegetable chopped up and seasoned with a sauce that contains a little coconut milk, a few tiny dried shrimp, chillies and many other unidentifiable ingredients. If you like very spicy dishes, the raw prawns (shrimp) with garlic, chilli and lemongrass will explode your taste buds. The pleasure lies in the contrast of the sweet prawn (shrimp) flesh and the fiery seasoning. The menu has a good repertoire of totally originally dishes as well as more classic ones – a mix of crispy, sweet, sour and spicy, it's quite addictive. The restaurant also has a plush interior, as is often the case in Thai restaurants, so why is it that Thai restaurants in France are often more chic and better decorated than Vietnamese, Cambodian or Chinese ones?

Opposite: The owners welcome their customers to a plush interior and serve, for example, beef marinated in lemongrass and chilli, one of the dishes prepared by the two restaurant chefs.

CRISPY PRAWNS WITH TAMARIND SAUCE

SERVES 4

Preparation: 35 min • **Cooking time:** 35 min

---

1 bunch of coriander (cilantro)

1 leek (just the white part)

1 sweet onion

2 garlic cloves

12 large prawns (shrimp)

1 tbsp caster (superfine) sugar

4 tbsp rice vinegar

100ml (3½fl oz/scant ½ cup) tamarind sauce

4 tbsp sweet (Thai) soy sauce

3 tbsp nuoc-mâm

80g (3oz/⅔ cup) cornflour (cornstarch)

cooking oil

Rinse and dry the coriander (cilantro), then set aside in a cool place. Rinse, dry and slice the leek into thin strips. Peel and chop the onion and garlic, then carefully peel the prawns (shrimp), keeping the heads and tails on.

Heat a little oil in a wok. When the oil is smoking, add the onion, garlic and sugar and brown for 2 minutes. Pour in the vinegar and bring to the boil before adding the tamarind sauce, soy sauce and nuoc-mâm. Cook for 5 minutes, then turn off the heat and keep warm. The sauce should reduce slightly and be quite thick.

Prepare and heat a deep-fryer. Carefully add the leek to the hot oil and deep-fry for 2 minutes. Drain on kitchen paper (paper towels).

Dip the prawns (shrimp) in the cornflour (cornstarch) and deep-fry them three at a time for 5 minutes, shaking regularly. Remove with a slotted spoon, drain on kitchen paper (paper towels) and arrange on a large plate. Pour over the tamarind sauce, sprinkle over the fried leek and and garnish with the coriander (cilantro) . Serve immediately.

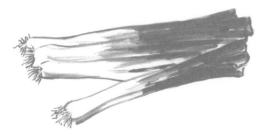

'NEMS'
SPRING ROLLS
SERVES 12

Preparation: 1 hr • **Cooking time:** 40 min

130g (4¾oz) rice vermicelli

5 dried black mushrooms

200g (7oz/2 cups) bean sprouts

1 sweet onion

1 large carrot

500g (1lb 2oz) minced
(ground) pork

1 egg

2 tbsp nuoc-mâm

22 large rice sheets

a few lettuce and
mint leaves

cooking oil

For the sauce:

8 tbsp nuoc-mâm

8 tbsp water

2 tbsp caster (superfine) sugar

2 tbsp rice vinegar

1 garlic clove, chopped

1 small chilli, sliced

Soak the vermicelli in a bowl of warm water for 20 minutes, then drain, squeeze and cut into small pieces with scissors. Soak the mushrooms for 15 minutes in a bowl of warm water then drain and cook them for a few minutes in a pan of boiling water. Drain and chop. Blanch the bean sprouts and set aside. Peel and chop the onion and peel and grate the carrot.

Put the minced (ground) pork into a bowl with the bean sprouts, carrot, mushrooms, vermicelli, egg and nuoc-mâm and use your hands to mix everything together thoroughly. Soften a sheet of rice paper by leaving it for 3–4 minutes between two tea (dish) towels soaked in warm water. Place a large spoonful of the filling into the middle of a rice sheet, then fold the edges over the filling and roll up tightly. Repeat until you have used up all the filling. Leave the rolls to dry at room temperature for 20 minutes.

Mix all the sauce ingredients together in a bowl and set aside. Prepare and heat a deep-fryer. Carefully drop the nems four at a time into the deep-fryer and deep-fry for 8–10 minutes, turning constantly. Remove with a slotted spoon and drain on kitchen paper (paper towels). Serve them hot and crispy, wrapped in a lettuce leaf with fresh mint leaves and dipped in the sauce.

CHINESE DUMPLINGS

Chinese dumplings are small bite-sized parcels made of rice dough that are steam-cooked and usually served in small bamboo baskets. In the last five or six years they have become very fashionable in the West, particularly in London, Paris, New York and Melbourne, where restaurants offering nothing but dumplings have opened up.

DUMPLINGS & OTHER BITE-SIZED DISHES

Originally from South China, dim sum are the typical Sunday meal in Hong Kong. They are eaten in the same way as a brunch, when families or friends get together at the weekend before midday for a meal that continues into the afternoon. Eating dim sum is a shared experience, but it's also the occasion to drink tea. In China this practice is called *yam'tcha*. In the West, eating dim sum doesn't have the same connotation and so lacks this relaxing family atmosphere. They are eaten for lunch or dinner in specialist or 'Chinese' restaurants where they are offered as starters. Be they *wonton*, *jiaozi* or *hakao*, dim sum come in multiple shapes and with a great variety of fillings. *Baozi*, on the other hand, are a kind of large white brioche filled with meat or vegetables. They may be sweet and filled with red bean purée, and they, too, are steam-cooked.

A stack of smoking-hot steaming baskets

Dumplings ready to cook
at restaurant 456

A basket or homemade dim sum at Vang's

Utensils for draining vegetables after cooking
them in a wok

41

SUI MAI

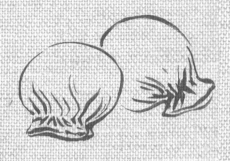

HA KAO

DIM SUM

BAOZI

MOCHI

JIAOZI

JIAN DUI

'BAOZI' STUFFED BUNS

SERVES 4-6

Preparation: 1 hr 10 min • Resting time: 2 hr

Cooking time: 30 min

For the dough:
400g (14oz/3¼ cups) wheat flour
3 packets bakers' yeast
100ml (3½fl oz/scant ½ cup)
warm water
100ml (3½fl oz/scant ½ cup)
warm milk
2 tsp caster (superfine) sugar
1 tbsp sesame oil
1 tbsp groundnut (peanut) oil
(+ 2 tbsp for cooking)

For the filling:
4 dried black mushrooms
250g (9oz) Chinese cabbage
500g (1lb 2oz) pork loin
30g (1oz) piece ginger
1 garlic clove
2 tbsp oyster sauce
salt and pepper

For the garnish:
2 spring onion (scallion) stems
1 tbsp white sesame seeds

For the sauce:
6 tbsp black Chinese vinegar
30g (1oz) piece ginger, peeled
and grated

To make the dough, in a bowl, mix the flour and yeast with the water, milk and sugar. Add the sesame oil and the 1 tbsp groundnut (peanut) oil and knead it together. Cover with clingfilm (plastic wrap) and leave for 2 hours at room temperature.

To make the filling, soak the mushrooms in a bowl of warm water for 15 minutes, then drain. Chop the cabbage finely and blanch for 1 minute in a pan of boiling water. User a mixer to mince (grind) the pork, cabbage, mushrooms, ginger and peeled garlic. Add the oyster sauce, salt and pepper.

Divide the dough into portions and roll out into small 10-cm (4-inch) circles. Place a dollop of the filling in the middle of each one. Enclose the filling by folding the dough up and over it, forming small pleats to make sure it is tightly sealed. Put the buns onto a piece of lightly greased baking parchment and place inside a steaming basket, then set the basket over a pan of boiling water and cook for 20 minutes.

When the buns are cooked and still hot, flash-fry them in a large pan with the 2 tbsp groundnut (peanut) oil. The buns should be browned and the bases slightly caramelized. Arrange them on a large plate and scatter over the snipped spring onions (scallions) and sesame seeds. Serve immediately with the sauce made of vinegar and ginger.

'HA KAO' PRAWN DUMPLINGS

SERVES 6

Preparation: 40 min • **Cooking time:** 15 min

For the filling:
400g (14oz) raw prawns (shrimp)
1 tsp sesame oil
2 tbsp soy sauce
1 pinch of caster (superfine)
sugar
1 tsp cornflour (cornstarch)
1 tbsp rice vinegar

1 egg white
60g (2oz) bamboo shoots

For the dough:
250g (9oz/2 cups) special
ha kao flour
250ml (9fl oz/generous 1 cup)
boiling water

For the sauce:
6 tbsp black Chinese vinegar
3 tbsp soy sauce
30g (1oz) piece ginger, peeled
and grated

To make the filling, peel the prawns (shrimp), then chop half of them into small pieces with a knife and put the rest into a food mixer with the sesame oil, soy sauce, sugar, cornflour (cornstarch), vinegar and egg white. You should get a smooth filling. Tip the filling into a bowl and mix with the roughly chopped bamboo shoots and the pieces of prawn (shrimp). Keep chilled.

To make the dough, pour the flour into a large bowl, add the boiling water a little at a time, stirring thoroughly with a wooden spatula, until you have a smooth dough. Form small balls of dough weighing about 13g (½oz) each, then flatten each ball into a small disc about 13cm (5 inches) in diameter. Place a spoonful of the filling in the middle of each one and fold the edges of the dough over the filling, making little pleats to form a purse-like shape.

Cook the dumplings in a steaming basket set over a pan of boiling water for about 15 minutes. You can line the base of the basket with greaseproof (wax) paper to prevent the dumplings sticking.

To make the sauce, mix all the ingredients together. Use chopsticks to dip the dumplings in the sauce before you eat them.

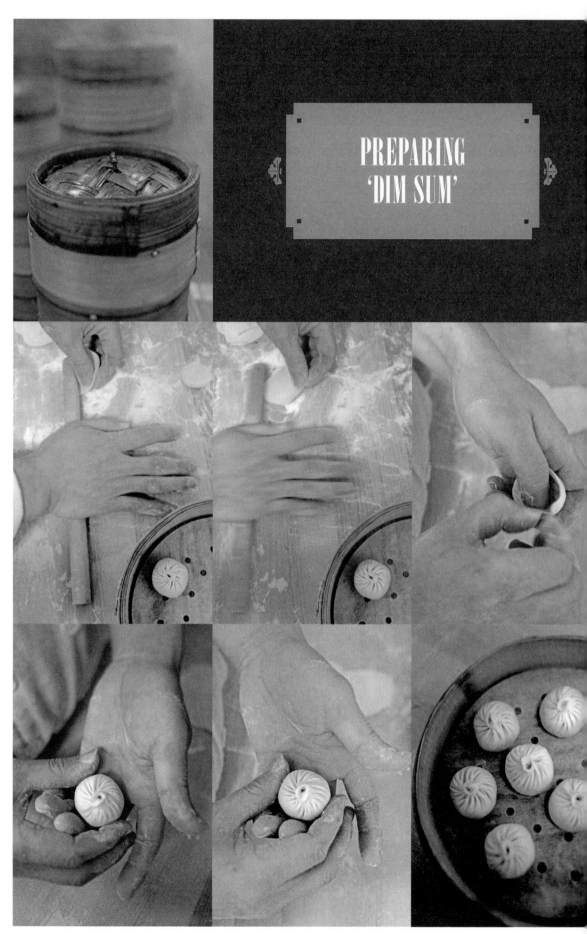

PREPARING 'DIM SUM'

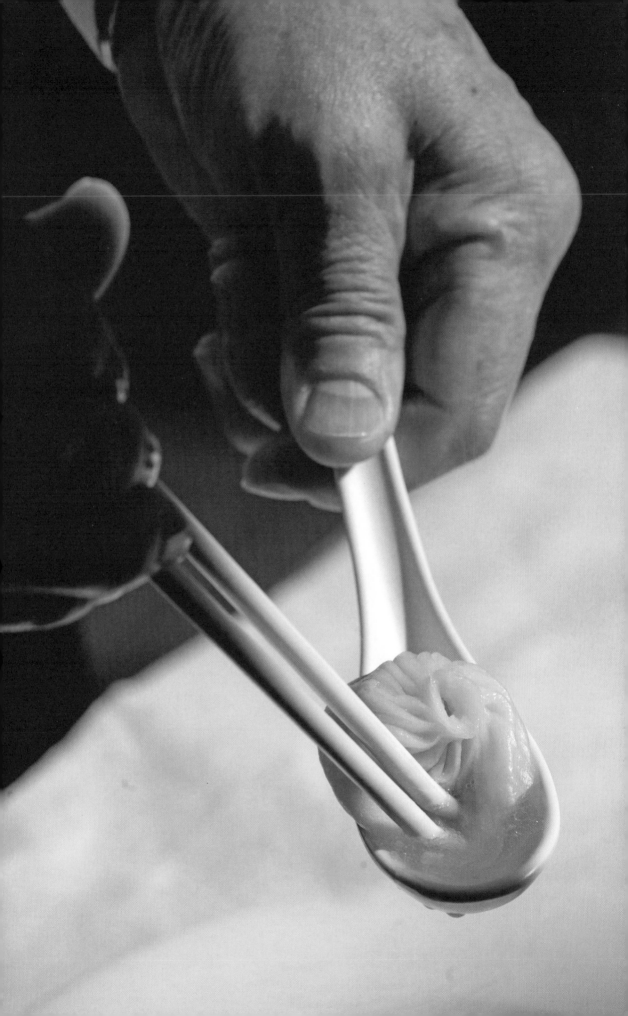

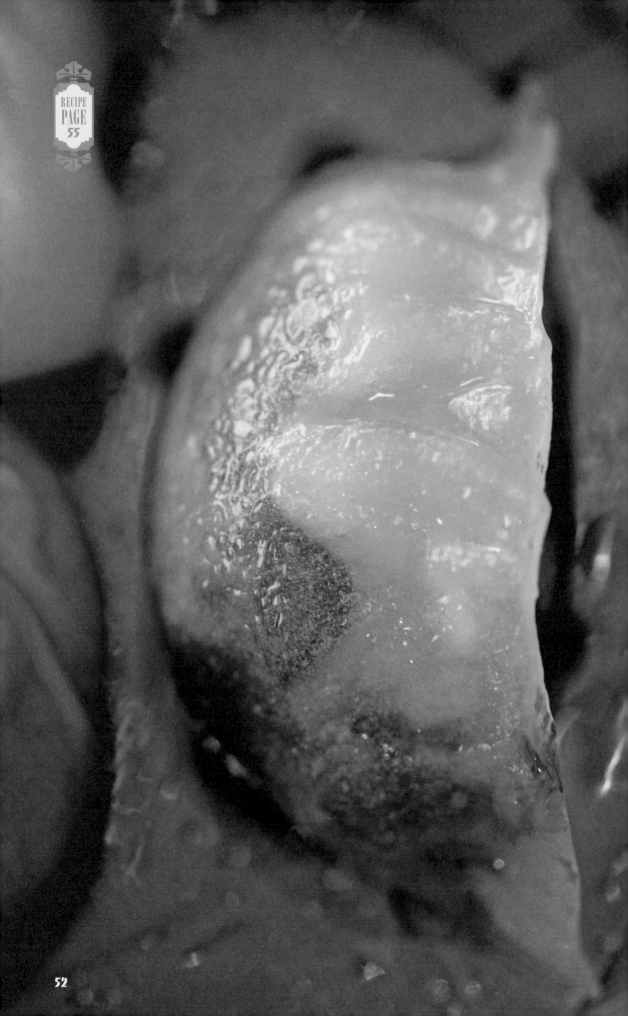

JUICY PORK DUMPLINGS

P. 50 • SERVES 6–8

Preparation: 1 hr • **Chilling time:** overnight

Cooking time: 20 min

For the jelly: 3 gelatine sheets, 160ml (5½fl oz/⅔ cup) beef stock (use remains of a beef casserole or a stock cube), 5g (⅛oz) piece ginger
For the filling: 300g (10½oz) pork loin, 4 spring onion (scallion) stems, 20g (¾oz) piece ginger, 50ml (2fl oz/scant ¼ cup) water, 2 tbsp Chinese wine, 2 tbsp Chinese soy sauce, 1 tbsp sesame oil, ½ tsp salt, 1 tsp caster (superfine) sugar, 1 tsp ground black pepper
For the dough: 230g (8½oz/scant 2 cups) flour, 130ml (4½fl oz/generous ½ cup) warm water
For the sauce: 6 tbsp black Chinese vinegar, 3 tbsp soy sauce, 30g (1oz) ginger, grated

Soften the gelatine in a bowl of cold water. Bring the stock to the boil with the peeled, sliced ginger and simmer for 5 minutes. Turn off the heat, add the gelatine and beat until dissolved. Pour the jelly into a container and chill overnight. Cut into cubes.

For the filling, cut the meat into pieces then use a mincer (grinder) or food mixer to mince finely. Rinse and chop the spring onions (scallions). Peel and grate the ginger. Put the meat in a bowl, add the spring onions (scallions), ginger, water, wine, soy sauce, sesame oil, salt, sugar and pepper and mix.
For the dough, put the flour in a bowl, make a well in the middle and pour in the warm water. Mix together gradually with your fingers. Knead the dough for several minutes then work it again with a rolling pin for another 5 minutes, folding and stretching it out several times. Divide the dough into 40 small balls. Flatten each ball into a small disc, about 8cm (3¼ inches) in diameter. Place a little of the stuffing in the middle of each disc and add two or three gelatine cubes. Fold the edges of the dough over the filling, pleating slightly as you do so to make a parcel. Cook the dumplings in a steamer basket for 15 minutes. Serve piping hot with chopsticks to dip the dumplings in the sauce and a spoon to scoop up the juices.

PRAWN AND SPINACH DUMPLINGS

P. 52 • SERVES 4

Preparation: 1 hr • **Resting time:** 1 hr

Cooking time: 20 min

For the dough: 60g (2¼oz/⅓ cup) potato starch, 125g (4½oz/1¼ cups) wheat starch, 250ml (9fl oz/generous 1 cup) boiling water, 1 tbsp lard
For the filling: 300g (10½oz) raw prawns (shrimp), 50g (1¾oz) pork, 100g (3½oz) spinach, 1 tbsp groundnut (peanut) oil, 1 tbsp soy sauce, 1 tsp sesame oil, 1 egg white, ½ tsp salt, a pinch of pepper
For the sauce: 6 tbsp black Chinese vinegar, 30g (1oz) grated ginger

For the dough, mix the starches together in a bowl, add the boiling water and beat with a wooden spoon until you have a smooth paste. Roll out the dough, place the lard in the middle and knead until well mixed. Cover with clingfilm (plastic wrap) and chill for 1 hour.

For the filling, peel the prawns (shrimp) and cut the pork into pieces. Strip the leaves from the spinach and rinse and dry them. Heat the groundnut (peanut) oil in a pan, add the spinach and stir for 1 minute, then drain and chop roughly. Use a food mixer to mince (grind) the pork, then add the prawns (shrimp), soy sauce, sesame oil, egg white, salt and pepper and mix until smooth. Shape the mixture into small balls weighing about 13g (½oz) each. Flatten each one into a small cushion shape. Place a little spinach and a little of the filling in the middle of each one, then close the dumplings into half moon shapes by folding the dough over the filling. Make little pleats around the edges to seal the dough firmly, then cook the dumplings in a steamer basket for about 15 minutes. Serve with chopsticks to dip them in the sauce.

456
SHANG HAI CUISINE

New York

69 MOTT ST.

SHANG HAI CUISINE

In the Chinatown district of Manhattan, it's an institution, a culinary temple that has been open since time immemorial – or at any rate for at least 40 years. The establishment has moved over the years but the cuisine has continued to titillate taste buds. The chef is from Shanghai and on the menu is *xiao long bao*: dumplings made with transparent dough and a juicy filling of either pork or, slightly more elaborate, pork and prawns (shrimp). (The Chinese like mixing styles, as long as they are edible.) These dumplings, steamed in their bamboo baskets, enclose a little meat stock as well as their filling. You eat them in one mouthful, or you run the risk of staining your shirt and losing the rich, tasty liquid that could have been obtained only in the most orthodox of ways: by boiling pork bones for several hours. The copious menu also offers fried noodles and cold sesame noodles, all of which encourages you to eat beyond your appetite in a bid to sample everything. But there's a long list of dishes – probably more than you could eat in a lifetime!

Opposite: The chef, who owns the restaurant, personally cooks all the specials, such as this dish of spinach sautéed with garlic, at the last minute.

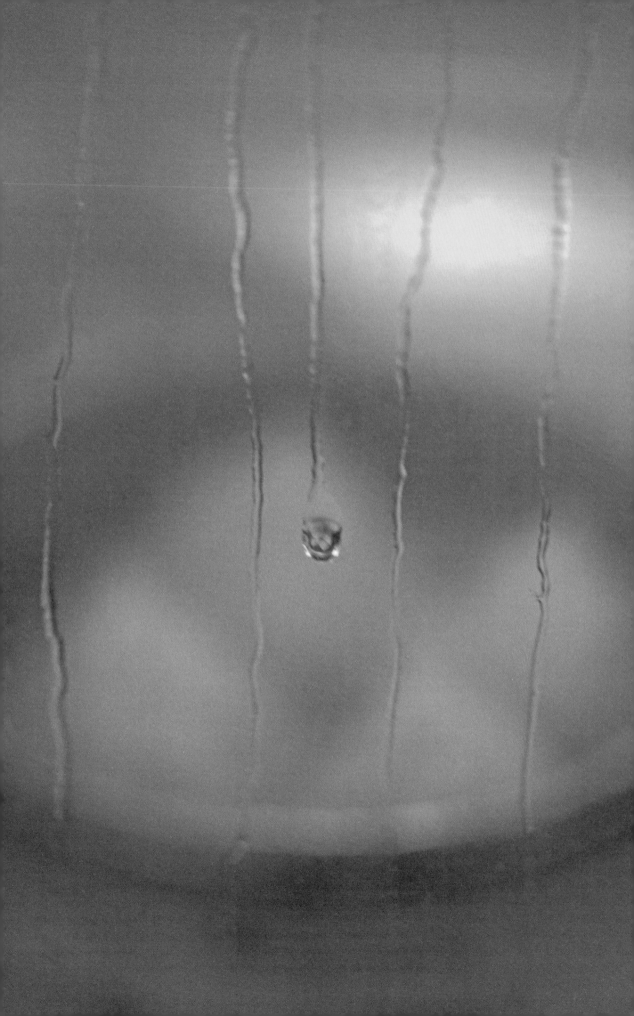

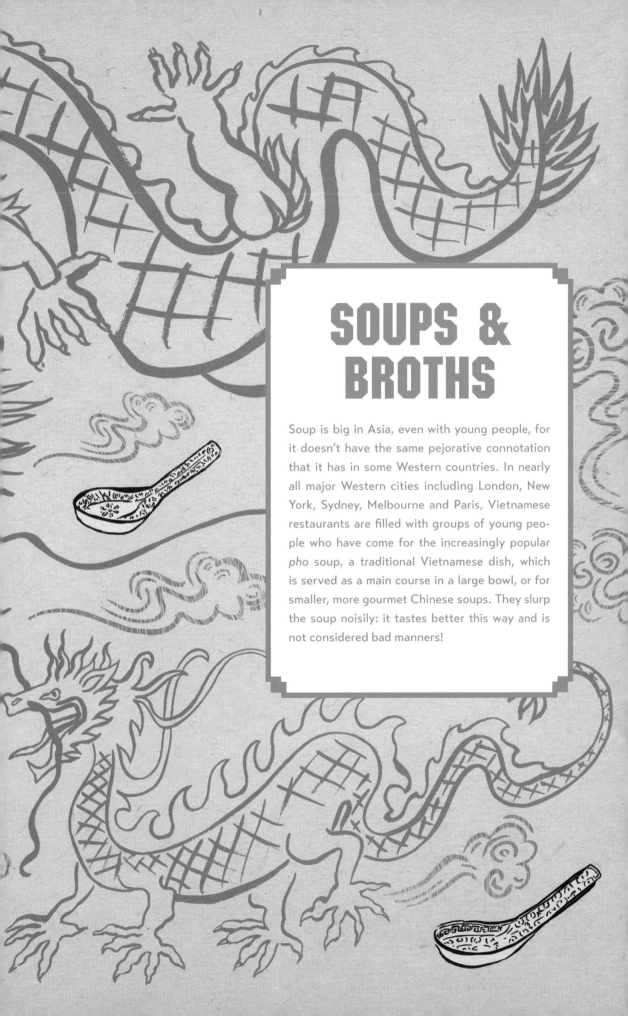

SOUPS & BROTHS

Soup is big in Asia, even with young people, for it doesn't have the same pejorative connotation that it has in some Western countries. In nearly all major Western cities including London, New York, Sydney, Melbourne and Paris, Vietnamese restaurants are filled with groups of young people who have come for the increasingly popular *pho* soup, a traditional Vietnamese dish, which is served as a main course in a large bowl, or for smaller, more gourmet Chinese soups. They slurp the soup noisily: it tastes better this way and is not considered bad manners!

SOUP

The most famous Asian soup in the West is the Vietnamese *pho*. It is made from a fragrant meat broth, long, flat rice noodles and fine slices of raw beef, which cook in the broth. Just before serving, fresh herbs, bean sprouts and lemon juice are added, as well as hoisin sauce, a thick, dark sauce made of soy beans, sugar, water, vinegar and spices. The soup is well stirred and served piping hot with a spoon and chopsticks.

In Vietnamese dishes, which have a reputation for being fresh and light, last-minute additions are common. In a *my tho* soup, which comes from Southern Vietnam, noodles, herbs, pork or prawns (shrimp) are served in a large bowl with broth on the side, which you pour over the soup yourself. Chinese restaurants also serve a whole range of broths garnished with prawn (shrimp) dumplings (wontons), roast meat (duck or pork), fish or seafood balls and noodles. These soups are a meal in themselves. Chinese restaurants also have a tradition of less substantial soups that provide just one element of a meal, such as the famous shark's fin soup, a gourmet dish that was served in the past at special feasts. (Today it is considered politically incorrect to eat shark's fin and is therefore rarely served.) Pekinese soup – a hot, sweet-and-sour soup with a mix of cartilaginous and sticky textures – is more widespread.

Though often ordered as starters in the West, soups in China are usually served during or at the end of a meal. Thai cuisine is full of soups that Westerners adore, such as *tom kha kaï*, a spicy soup made with coconut milk, lemongrass and chicken. There is also a huge range of fondue dishes in Asia, particularly in China, with the ingredients of the broth varying according to the region.

*Garnish for pho soup in the kitchens of
Dong Huang restaurant*

Bowls ready for Pho soup

A neon sign in this New York restaurant
indicates that hot soup is served
24 hours a day

Garnishing the piping hot pho
broth to order

69

PEKINESE SOUP

SERVES 4–6

Preparation: 35 min • **Cooking time:** 30 min

5 dried black mushrooms

2 chicken breasts

3 spring onion (scallion) stems

5 coriander (cilantro) sprigs

1 red (bell) pepper

1 egg

2 tsp sesame oil

3 tbsp cornflour
(cornstarch)

1 small can of bamboo shoots

60g (2¼oz) fresh tofu

1 tbsp vegetable oil

1.5 litres (2½ pints/6⅓ cups)
chicken stock

5 tbsp soy sauce

3 tbsp rice vinegar

1 dash of chilli paste

Soak the mushrooms in a bowl of warm water for 15 minutes, or until soft, then drain, squeeze them out and chop them. Steam the chicken breasts for 15 minutes, then chop.

Rinse the spring onions (scallions) and coriander (cilantro) and snip finely with scissors. Set aside. Deseed the pepper and chop finely. Beat the egg with the sesame oil. Whisk the cornflour (cornstarch) with a little water, then drain the bamboo shoots and chop. Cut the tofu into small pieces.

Heat the vegetable oil in a wok. Brown the chicken, pepper, mushrooms and bamboo shoots in the hot oil for 5 minutes. Pour over the stock, soy sauce and vinegar, bring to the boil then add the tofu, chilli paste and cornflour (cornstarch) mixture and cook for about 7 minutes, or until thick. Turn off the heat.

Add the beaten egg and bring back to the boil for 1 minute, stirring with chopsticks. Remove from the heat and pour the soup into bowls. Sprinkle with the spring onion (scallion) and coriander (cilantro), stir again and enjoy.

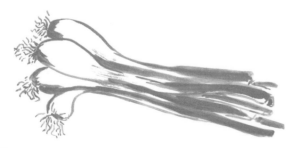

FISH BROTH WITH FISH DUMPLINGS

SERVES 4

Preparation: 45 min • **Cooking time:** 1 hr 30 min

10 spring onion (scallion) stems
30g (1oz) piece galangal
3 lemongrass stalks
1 onion

2 garlic cloves
1kg (2¼lb) fish heads and bones
2 tbsp groundnut (peanut) oil
2 tsp cane sugar

6 tbsp nuoc-mâm
1 tsp *prahok* (fish paste)
12 dumplings or frozen
fish balls

Rinse and snip the spring onions (scallions) with scissors amd set aside. Peel and slice the galangal, then peel and roughly chop the lemongrass. Peel and chop the onion and garlic. Break up the fish heads and bones.

Heat the oil in a large wok and stir-fry the onion and garlic in the hot oil. Leave them to sweat for a few minutes without browning then add the fish heads and bones, the lemongrass, sugar, galangal, nuoc-mâm and fish paste. Add 2 litres (3½ pints/8½ cups) water and bring to the boil. Stir then reduce the heat and leave to simmer for an hour.

Strain the fish stock into another saucepan and bring back to the boil before adding the dumplings or fish balls and cooking them for a few minutes. Divide among four serving bowls, sprinkle with the spring onions (scallions) and serve piping hot.

RECIPE
PAGE
79

'KWAY TEOW' PORK AND PRAWN SOUP

P. 74 • SERVES 4–6

Preparation: 45 min • **Cooking time:** 3 hr

For the broth: 1 onion, 50g (1¾oz) piece ginger, 700g (1lb 9oz) pork bones, 2 chicken carcasses, 2 celery stalks, 1 dried squid, 5 tbsp nuoc-mâm, 2 tsp cane sugar

For the garnish: ½ a bunch of coriander (cilantro), 4 spring onion (scallion) stems, 200g (7oz) pork shoulder, 20 prawns (shrimp), 100g (3½oz) cooked roast pork or *cha lua* (a kind of Vietnamese mortadella), 200g (7oz/2 cups) bean sprouts, 300g (10½oz) vermicelli or rice *hu tieu* noodles, 12 fish balls, juice of 2 limes

For the broth, peel the onion, chop into small pieces and brown in a pan. Peel the ginger and slice thickly. Put the pork bones and chicken carcasses into a large pan, cover with water and bring to the boil. Drain and wash the bones. Clean the pan and put the bones back in. Add the browned onion, ginger, chopped celery stalks, dried squid, nuoc-mâm and sugar, then pour over 3.5 litres (6 pints/3¾ quarts) of water and bring to the boil. Reduce the heat and simmer over a very low heat for 2 hours 30 minutes.

For the garnish, rinse, dry and chop the coriander (cilantro) and spring onions (scallions). Chop the pork shoulder. Peel the prawns (shrimp) and slice the roast pork into thin pieces. Drop the bean sprouts into boiling water for 1 minute, then drain and set aside. Strain the broth into a large saucepan and bring back to the boil. Cook the vermicelli or the noodles in the broth then divide them among the bowls. Next, cook the prawns (shrimp) for 3 minutes in the broth, then add the fish balls, roast pork slices, chopped pork and bean sprouts. Add a good amount of hot broth to the bowls, sprinkle over the spring onions (scallions) and coriander (cilantro), add lime juice and serve the soup piping hot.

BROTH WITH WONTON DUMPLINGS

P. 75 • SERVES 4

Preparation: 1 hr • **Cooking time:** 2 hr

For the broth: 2 chicken carcasses, 3 garlic cloves, 4 small spring onions (scallions), 30g (1oz) piece ginger, 50g (1¾oz) dried black mushrooms, soaked in warm water for 15 minutes, coarse salt
For the dumplings: 4 spring onions (scallions), 200g (7oz) lean pork, 1 tsp sesame oil, 1 egg yolk, 3 tbsp soy sauce, 50g (1¾oz) shrimps, 40 Chinese wonton wrappers, salt and pepper

For the broth, break up the chicken carcasses, put them in a large pan and pour over 2 litres (3½ pints/8½ cups) water. Smash the unpeeled garlic cloves and add these, the onions and the peeled and sliced ginger and simmer over a low heat for 2 hours. Strain the broth into a clean pan (you should have about 1 litre/1¾ pints/4 cups) and add the mushrooms. Keep warm.
Meanwhile, chop the spring onions (scallions) with the pork and mix with the sesame oil, egg yolk and soy sauce. Peel the prawns (shrimps), add them to the filling and season. Place a wonton square in the palm of your hand. Add 1 tsp of the filling, then fold over to form a triangle. Press down and pinch the edges to seal tightly. Cook the dumplings for 10 minutes in a pan of boiling water. Divide the dumplings among four bowls, pour over the hot broth and serve.

CHINESE FONDUE

P. 77 • SERVES 6

Preparation: 25 min • **Cooking time:** 10 min

200g (7oz) Chinese cabbage, 200g (7oz) broccoli, 100g (3½oz) shiitake mushrooms, 200g (7oz) beef, 20 prawns (shrimp), 2 litres (3½ pints/8½ cups) beef stock, 2 tbsp soy sauce, 1 tbsp sweet-and-sour chilli sauce

Chop the vegetables into small pieces, slice the beef thinly and peel the prawns (shrimp). Bring the stock to the boil, then add the soy sauce and sweet-and-sour sauce, whisking as you go. Reduce for 10 minutes then pour the broth into a fondue pan.
Serve with little metal baskets to use for dipping the beef, prawns (shrimp) or vegetables into the broth for cooking.

CHICKEN SOUP WITH NOODLES

SERVES 6–8

Preparation: 45 min • **Cooking time:** 3 hr

2 large onions
100g (3½oz) piece ginger
2 tbsp groundnut (peanut) oil
4 star anise
1 cinnamon stick
10 coriander seeds

2 plump chickens, about 1.2kg
(2lb 12oz) each, cut into pieces
6 litres (10½ pints/5¼ quarts)
water
5 tbsp nuoc-mâm
1 tbsp salt

1 tbsp cane sugar
10 spring onion (scallion) stems
6 sticks of *yu choy sum*
(oilseed rape or Chinese
flowering cabbage)
500g (1lb 2oz) *banh pho* noodles

Peel and finely chop the onions, then rinse, peel and slice the ginger. Heat the oil in a large saucepan, add the dried spices and let them roast for 4 minutes. Remove them with a slotted spoon and set aside.

Next, stir-fry the onions, ginger and chicken in the oil for 5 minutes until brown. Add a little water, then the spices, nuoc-mâm, salt and pepper, and bring to the boil. Skim, reduce the heat to low and simmer for 2 hours. Rinse and chop the spring onions (scallions) and set aside. Strain the broth and reserve the chicken, then bring the broth back to the boil in a pan.

Rinse the Chinese cabbage and stir-fry for 5 minutes in a wok. Cook the noodles for a few minutes in the broth, then drain and divide among four large bowls. Add some pieces of chicken and the Chinese cabbage, stems cut in half, then pour over the boiling broth. Sprinkle with the spring onions (scallions) and enjoy.

CRAB AND ASPARAGUS SOUP

SERVES 4–6

Preparation: 25 min • **Cooking time:** 25 min

400g (14oz) green asparagus

3 tbsp cornflour (cornstarch)

3 coriander (cilantro) sprigs

1 litre (1¾ pints/4 cups) chicken stock (see recipe for broth with wonton dumplings on p.79)

1 x 240g (8½oz) can crabmeat

1 tbsp nuoc-mâm

2 egg whites

Trim the asparagus spears, cut in half and cook for a few minutes in a saucepan of boiling water. Keep the tips whole and slice the stems.

Whisk the cornflour (cornstarch) with a little water and set aside. Rinse and chop the coriander (cilantro) and reserve.

Heat the stock in a wok then add the asparagus pieces, crabmeat and nuoc-mâm. Bring to the boil and pour in the cornflour (cornstarch) mixture, stirring all the time.

When the soup has thickened, turn off the heat. Whisk the egg whites and stir them slowly into the soup using chopsticks until they start to set. Pour the soup into bowls, sprinkle with coriander (cilantro) and serve hot.

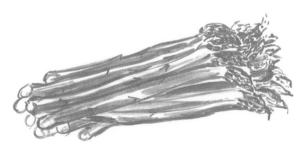

RECIPE
PAGE
89

'HU TIEU' SOUP WITH QUAIL'S EGGS

P. 85 • SERVES 6

Preparation: 45 min • **Cooking time:** 2 hr 30 min

For the broth: 1 onion, 50g (1¾oz) piece ginger, 700g (1lb 9oz) pork bones, 2 chicken carcasses, 2 celery stalks, 1 dried squid, 5 tbsp nuoc-mâm, 2 tsp cane sugar

For the garnish: 1 bunch of coriander (cilantro), 4 spring onion (scallion) stems, 2 squid, 2 tbsp groundnut (peanut) oil, 12 large prawns (shrimp), 300g (10½oz) glazed pork, 100g (3½oz/1 cup) bean sprouts, 4 baby leeks, 12 boiled quail's eggs, 300g (10½oz) rice noodles, juice of 2 limes, 4 tbsp fish sauce

Peel and chop the onion then brown it in a frying pan. Peel the ginger and cut into thick slices. Put the pork bones and chicken carcasses into a large pan, cover with water and bring to the boil. Drain and wash the bones. Put the bones back into the cleaned pan and add the onion, ginger, chopped celery, squid, nuoc-mâm and sugar. Pour in 3.5 litres (6 pints/3¾ quarts) water and bring to the boil, then reduce the heat to low and simmer for 2 hours 30 minutes.
Meanwhile, prepare the garnish. Rinse the coriander (cilantro), then rinse and chop the spring onions (scallions). Empty the squid and chop into rings, then fry for 5 minutes in the oil. Peel the prawns (shrimp) and poach for 2 minutes in the broth. Cut the pork into thin slices. Blanch the bean sprouts for 2 minutes in the broth. Rinse and cut the leeks in half and brown for 2 minutes in the pan. Divide the quail's eggs, bean sprouts, squid, prawns (shrimp), leeks, pork, coriander (cilantro) and spring onions (scallions) among six bowls. Drop the noodles into the broth for 3–4 minutes, then strain the broth into separate bowls. Serve with the prawns (shrimp), mixing a little broth with a little garnish. Season with lime and fish sauce.

'TOM KAÏ' KATHAI CHICKEN SOUP WITH COCONUT MILK

P. 84 • SERVES 4–6

Preparation: 35 min • **Cooking time:** 25 min

2 limes, 1 small red chilli (optional), 300g (10½oz) piece fresh galangal or 100g (3½oz) dried galangal, soaked in water for 30 minutes, 1 bunch of coriander (cilantro), 2 boned chicken thighs, 2 chicken breasts, 4 kaffir lime leaves, 3 lemongrass stalks, 2 x 250g (9oz) cartons coconut milk, 1 x 250g (9oz) carton creamed coconut, 3 tbsp ground galangal, 3 tbsp fish sauce, salt and pepper

Squeeze the limes, slice the chilli, peel the fresh or dried galangal and cut into thin slices. Rinse and dry the coriander (cilantro), remove the leaves from the stalks and chop the stalks finely. Arrange the chicken, galangal, coriander (cilantro) stalks, kaffir lime leaves and peeled and chopped lemongrass in a large pan, add the coconut milk and bring to the boil. Reduce the heat and simmer gently for 20 minutes, stirring regularly. Add the creamed coconut, ground galangal, fish sauce, lime juice, chilli and coriander (cilantro) leaves. Stir and season to taste. Serve piping hot.

SWEET-AND-SOUR CHINESE SOUP

P. 87 • SERVES 4

Preparation: 25 min • **Cooking time:** 15 min

6 dried black mushrooms, 50g (1¾oz) piece ginger, 1 x 250g (9oz) can bamboo shoots, 4 spring onion (scallion) stems, 1 tbsp cornflour (cornstarch), 200g (7oz) cooked duck (from Chinese food stores), 2 tbsp groundnut (peanut) oil, ½ tsp dried chilli, 1 tbsp rice wine, 800ml (1⅓ pints/ 3½ cups) chicken stock, 2 tbsp soy sauce, 1 tsp five-spice, 2 tsp cane sugar, 2 tbsp white rice wine, 1 egg

Soak the mushrooms for 15 minutes in a bowl of warm water, then squeeze dry and chop. Peel and chop the ginger, then drain and chop the bamboo shoots. Rinse and snip the spring onions (scallions) with scissors. Whisk the cornflour (cornstarch) with a little water and set aside. Cut the duck into small pieces. Heat the oil in a large wok and stir-fry the ginger then add the mushrooms and stir-fry for 2 minutes. Add the chilli and rice wine, allow to reduce a little before adding the stock, bamboo shoots, soy sauce, five-spice, sugar and rice vinegar. Bring to the boil and cook for 5 minutes. Whisk in the cornflour (cornstarch) mixture. Once the soup has thickened, turn off the heat and gradually add the beaten egg, mixing with a fork as you go. Pour the soup into bowls, add the pieces of duck, sprinkle with spring onion (scallion) and serve.

BO KY

New York

Vietnamese food has a very different taste in the West, where it's what we call the cuisine of immigration – it adapts itself to the countries where it is found. The Bo Ky restaurant in New York is run by Chinese from Vietnam and Cambodia and the result is a fusion of the two cultures. The Bo Ky bowls taste of both cultures and histories and the famous *teochew*-style fish and rice soup bears testimony to this. With such a name it clearly comes from China, but nonetheless it has all the characteristics of a Vietnamese soup. The restaurant indicates that it offers Chinese and Vietnamese cuisine, but the menu also includes numerous Cambodian dishes, such as the Cambodian-style rice noodles or the beef and tomato soup. The immigrants in the United States are like this, free and without borders, in their minds at least. For this alone, the place is worth the journey. We went there and the result: extremely good food at a very low price!

Opposite: The Bo Ky cook prepares the soups that will be served at breakfast.

PHO
SOUP

SERVES 4–6

Preparation: 45 min • **Cooking time:** 3 hr 30 min

1 red chilli	500g (1lb 2oz) beef brisket	400g (14oz) rice noodles
4 mint sprigs	400g (14oz) flank or	200g (7oz/2 cups) bean sprouts
4 coriander (cilantro) sprigs	plate of beef	100g (3½oz) lean beef
4 Thai basil sprigs	300g (10½oz) beef bones	(rump, sirloin, fillet,
3 spring onion (scallion) stems	2 black cardamom seeds	tenderloin)
50g (1¾oz) piece ginger	3 star anise	juice of 2 limes
2 shallots	1 cinnamon stick	nuoc-mâm, to season

Trim and slice the chilli and rinse and chop the herbs. Rinse and slice the spring onions (scallions), peel the ginger and cut it into pieces, then peel the shallots.

Place the beef (brisket and flank) and beef bones into a large pan, cover with water and bring to the boil. Drain the meat and bones then rinse them under cold running water.

Put the meat and bones back into the cleaned pan and add the shallots, ginger, cardamom, star anise and cinnamon. Cover with water to 10cm (4 inches) above the level of the ingredients, bring to the boil, then reduce the heat to low and simmer for 3 hours 30 minutes. Once the meat is cooked, drain and cut into small slices.

Cook the noodles for 3 minutes in a pan of boiling water then divide them among large bowls. Add the cooked meat, bean sprouts, some herbs, onion and chilli. Fill the bowls with the broth, cut the raw meat into thin slices and add this too. Season with lime juice and nuoc-mâm and serve.

PHO 99

Paris

A Vietnamese canteen full of Vietnamese customers: it's a good sign, as is the welcoming smile at the entrance when you arrive. If you feel like tasting authentic Vietnamese flavours in the heart of Paris, this is the address for you. The Vietnamese rice crêpe filled with pork and served with fresh herbs is a speciality, as is the *mi kho*, a dry stew from South Vietnam, complemented with pork and prawn (shrimp) noodles and accompanied by a broth served separately and poured in at the last moment. You can also enjoy more classic dishes, such as *pho* soup with its fresh herbs, *bo bun* and *bun cha*. Note that all the dishes on the menu are also available to take-away.

Opposite: This family restaurant, located at the heart of Parisian Chinatown, boasts *bun cha* as its speciality.

CHICKEN & QUAIL

鸡肉

進煌飯店

CANTON KITCHEN 171 INC. ☎ 34

CHICKEN

Chicken is a part of Asian cuisine and is used in all types of dishes, as the recipes in this chapter show. Note, however, that the Chinese also willingly eat chicken feet, which involves sucking the feet and the small bones as there isn't much meat, it's mainly cartilage and skin. Poultry is not butchered in the same way as it is in the West; it is simply chopped into rough pieces, and the bones are usually left in, to gnaw on! This is all part of the pleasure.

Chicken and rice is a great Singaporean speciality, but it originates from the island of Haînan in China. This relatively simple-looking dish is, in fact, quite complex.

Previous page: Roast duck hanging in the window of a New York restaurant..

It consists of a whole chicken cooked in broth with all kinds of seasonings, such as spring onions (scallions), coriander (cilantro), ginger or sometimes garlic, served with rice that has also been cooked in broth. The chicken is chopped into pieces, then arranged on, or beside, the rice, and the final dish is sprinkled with fresh coriander (cilantro) leaves. A bowl of broth accompanies it, as well as different sauces, which vary according to the region but most typically include a sauce with garlic and grated ginger marinated in oil.

Facade of a Chinese restaurant specializing in duck

Poached chickens drying for the preparation of Chicken and rice

Roast ducks hanging in a restaurant window

Fish balls cooking

CHICKEN AND RICE

SERVES 4-6

Preparation 1 hr • Cooking time: 1 hr 30 min

2 garlic cloves
30g (1oz) piece ginger
1 plump chicken,
about 1.2kg (2lb 12oz)
4 tbsp soy sauce
2 tsp sesame oil
1 bunch of coriander
(cilantro)

For the rice:
500g (1lb 2oz) fragrant rice
1 tsp goose fat
2 garlic cloves
1 small sweet onion
20g (¾oz) piece ginger

For the chilli sauce:
2 tbsp chilli sauce

½ tsp caster (superfine) sugar
juice of 2 limes

For the ginger sauce:
50g (1¾oz) piece ginger
1 tbsp groundnut (peanut) oil
1 spring onion (scallion) with its
stem, finely chopped

Crush the garlic with the skin on. Pour 2 litres (3½ pints/8½ cups) water into a large pan, add the finely sliced ginger and garlic then bring to the boil.

Wash the chicken under cold running water and scrape the skin with the pointed end of a knife. Remove the fat around the tail end and set aside. Drop the chicken into the boiling water, reduce the heat the low and cook for 30 minutes. Turn off the heat, cover the pan and let the chicken finish cooking like this for another 30 minutes.

Meanwhile, wash the rice several times in cold water until the water runs clear, then spread it out on a cloth to dry.

Melt the goose fat and reserved chicken fat in a wok, add the peeled and chopped garlic, onion and ginger and cook for 5 minutes, stirring regularly so they don't brown. Add the rice, stir and cook until the grains turn transparent. Pour over 650ml (1¼ pints/scant 3 cups) of the chicken broth and cover. Bring to the boil then reduce the heat to the minimum and cook for 8–10 minutes.

Turn off the heat and wait 5 minutes before removing the lid. Drain the chicken and baste it with the soy sauce and sesame oil. Wash, strip and dry the coriander (cilantro). Prepare the sauces by mixing the respective ingredients together.

Chop the chicken and arrange the pieces on a large plate. Sprinkle over the coriander (cilantro) leaves and serve with the hot rice, the broth in a bowl and the sauces in bowls on the side.

GENERAL TAO'S CHICKEN

P. 115 • SERVES 4

Preparation: 30 min • **Marinating time:** 1 hr

Cooking time: 25 min

1 large onion, 2 garlic cloves, 15g (½oz) piece ginger, 4 chicken breasts, 1 tsp dried chilli powder, 4 tbsp soy sauce, 2 tbsp tamarind sauce, 2 tbsp rice vinegar, 1 tbsp cornflour (cornstarch), 3 spring onion (scallion) stems, 1 tbsp sesame seeds, vegetable oil
For the sauce: 2 tbsp caster (superfine) sugar, 1 small glass of chicken stock, 1 tsp sesame oil, 2 tbsp soy sauce, 2 tbsp tamarind sauce

Peel and chop the onion and garlic, then peel and grate the ginger. Cut the chicken into small pieces then place in a bowl with the sauces, vinegar, cornflour (cornstarch), onion, garlic, ginger and chilli powder and leave to marinate at room temperature for 1 hour. Roughly chop the spring onions (scallions). About 20 minutes before serving, heat the oil in a large wok over a high heat. Add the chicken pieces to the smoking oil and brown for a few minutes. Add the sugar and let the chicken caramelize before pouring over the stock, sesame oil and sauces. Cook over a high heat until the sauce is reduced and thick, then add the spring onions (scallions). Mix then arrange in a serving dish. Sprinkle over the sesame seeds and serve with white rice.

SWEET-AND-SOUR CHICKEN WITH PINEAPPLE

P. 116 • SERVES 4

Preparation: 30 min • **Cooking time:** 40 min

4 boneless chicken thighs, 2 tbsp soy sauce, 1 large onion, 1 x 250g (9oz) can pineapple in syrup, 1 tbsp groundnut (peanut) oil, 2 tbsp cornflour (cornstarch), 3 tbsp rice vinegar, 250ml (9fl oz/generous 1 cup) tomato sauce, 3 tbsp caster (superfine) sugar, 2 tbsp oyster sauce, 2 garlic cloves, 300g (10½oz/scant 2½ cups) flour, cooking oil

Cut the chicken into small pieces, then leave to marinate in the soy sauce. Peel and roughly chop the onion, drain the pineapple (set the juice aside) and chop into small pieces. Heat the groundnut (peanut) oil in a wok, add the pineapple pieces and chopped onion and stir-fry until brown. Add the cornflour (cornstarch), stir then add the pineapple syrup, vinegar, tomato sauce, sugar, oyster sauce and chopped garlic. (You can substitute the tomato sauce and caster/superfine sugar with 4 tbsp ketchup if you wish.) Cook for 25 minutes, then set aside. Prepare and heat a deep-fryer. Drain the chicken and dip in the flour. Place the pieces into the hot oil and deep-fry for 5–8 minutes, shaking well to make sure they are brown and cooked. Drain and drop into the sweet-and-sour sauce. Cook for 5 minutes and serve with white rice.

STUFFED CHICKEN WINGS WITH VERMICELLI AND MUSHROOMS

P. 117 • SERVES 4

Preparation: 45 min • **Cooking time:** 25 min

10g (¼oz) dried black mushrooms, 20g (¾oz) soy vermicelli, 200g (7oz) sausage meat, 1 egg, 1 lemongrass stalk, 1 tbsp sesame oil, 3 tbsp nuoc-mâm, 4 large chicken wings, 1 bunch of coriander (cilantro), 2 garlic cloves, 1 tbsp groundnut (peanut) oil, cooking oil, 300g (10½oz/3 cups) bean sprouts, a little ginger
For the sauce: 2 tbsp nuoc-mâm, 2 tbsp warm water, 30g (1oz/2 tbsp) caster (superfine) sugar, 2 tbsp rice vinegar, juice of 1 lime, 1 small red chilli, finely chopped

Soak the mushrooms in a bowl of warm water for 15 minutes until soft. Drain and chop them finely. Cut the vermicelli into small pieces. In a large bowl, mix the sausage meat with the mushrooms, vermicelli, egg, chopped lemongrass, sesame oil and nuoc-mâm. Bone the chicken wings using the point of a knife to cut away the flesh without damaging the skin. Remove the bones. Stuff the wings with the sausage mixture and seal them by stitching the skin. Steam-cook the stuffed wings for 20 minutes then leave to cool. About 15 minutes before serving, mix the sauce ingredients together. Rinse, strip and dry the coriander (cilantro) and peel and chop the garlic. Heat the groundnut (peanut) oil in a wok and stir-fry the bean sprouts and garlic for a few minutes. Prepare and heat a deep-fryer. Carefully lower the chicken wings into the hot oil and deep-fry for a few minutes. Drain, cover in the sauce and serve with the bean sprouts and season with a little ginger.

QUAIL WITH FIVE-SPICE

SERVES 4

Preparation: 20 min • **Resting time:** 2 hr • **Cooking time:** 1 hr

4 quails
2 tbsp five-spice mixture
(+ 1 tbsp to serve)
1 garlic clove

½ tsp ground cumin
2 tbsp runny honey
5 tbsp soy sauce
juice of 1 lemon

a few coriander (cilantro) sprigs
salt and pepper

Baste the inside and outside of the quail with 1 tbsp of the five-spice mixture, then season with salt and pepper and set aside.

Peel and crush the garlic, then place in a mortar with the remaining five-spice mixture and the cumin. Crush to form a smooth paste, then stir in the honey and soy sauce. Baste the quail with this mixture and leave to dry for 2 hours at room temperature.

Preheat the oven to 160°C/325°F/Gas Mark 3. Place the quail in a large dish and cook in the oven for 1 hour, basting regularly with the spicy paste. The quail should be very well cooked, tender and caramel-coloured.

Cut the quail into pieces and serve with lemon juice, a few coriander (cilantro) leaves, a little more five-spice and white rice.

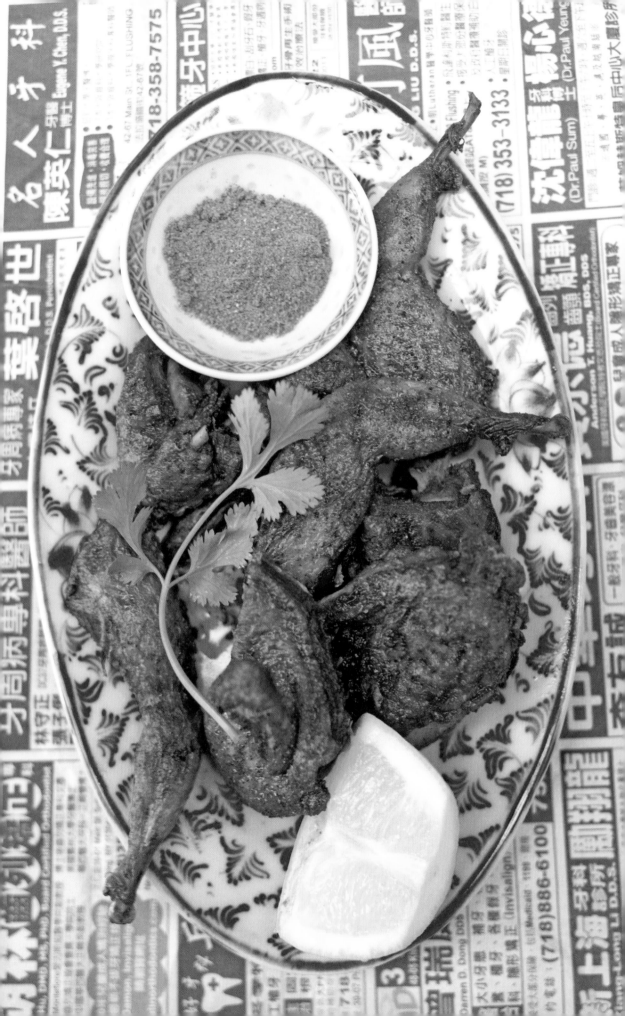

CHICKEN CURRY WITH AUBERGINE

SERVES 4

Preparation: 25 min • **Cooking time:** 1 hr

2 garlic cloves
1 onion
4 small ripe aubergines (eggplants)
2 courgettes (zucchini)

4 tbsp groundnut (peanut) oil
1 chicken, about 1.2kg (2lb 12oz), jointed
1 tbsp curry paste (strong or mild, according to taste)

100ml (3½fl oz/scant ½ cup) chicken stock
50ml (2fl oz/scant ¼ cup) coconut milk
10 Thai basil leaves

Peel and chop the garlic and onion, then trim the aubergines (eggplants) and courgettes (zucchini) and cut into large sticks.

Heat the groundnut (peanut) oil in a large wok. Add the garlic and onion to the hot oil and brown for 1 minute then add the chicken pieces, aubergine (eggplant) and courgette (zucchini). Mix and stir-fry for 5 minutes.

Add the curry paste then cover with the chicken stock and coconut milk. Leave to simmer over a low heat for 45 minutes.

Turn off the heat, add the basil, stir, then arrange in a shallow dish. Serve with white rice.

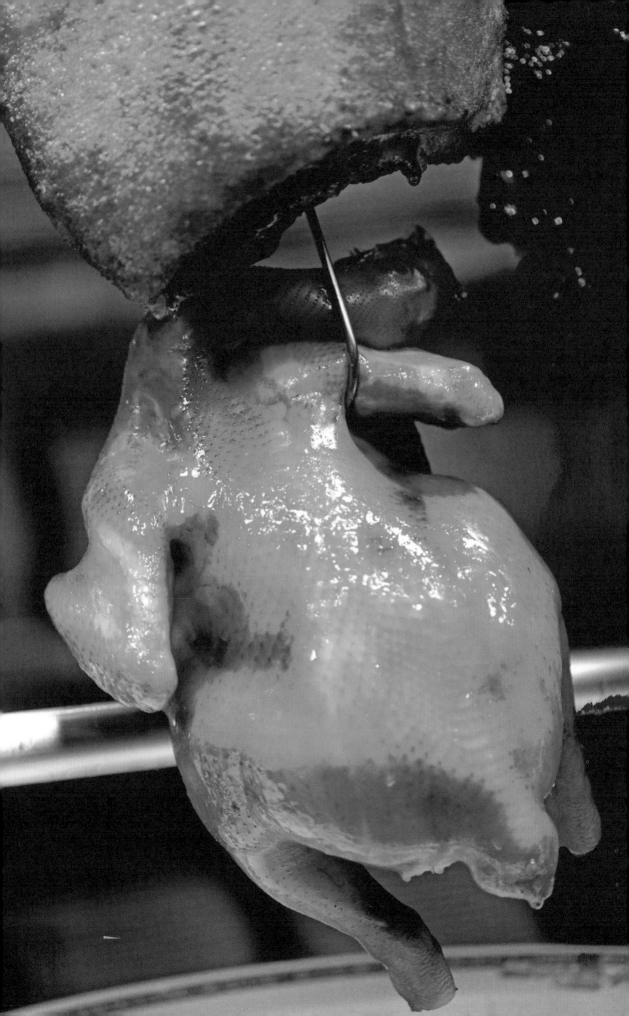

RECIPE
PAGE
130

CARAMELIZED CHICKEN WITH SESAME

P. 127 • SERVES 4

Preparation: 30 min • Marinating **time:** 1 hr

Cooking time: 25 min

4 boneless chicken thighs, 2 garlic cloves, 1 onion, 8 tbsp soy sauce, 2 tsp sesame oil, 1 tbsp rice vinegar, 10 sugar cubes, 1 tbsp cooking oil, 1 tbsp toasted sesame seeds

Cut the chicken into small pieces, then peel and chop the garlic and onion. Marinate the chicken with the garlic, onion, 4 tbsp soy sauce, 1 tsp sesame oil and the rice vinegar.

Put the sugar cubes into a pan with 1 tbsp water and leave them to caramelize into a light brown caramel. Remove from the heat then stir in the remaining soy sauce and sesame oil using a wooden spoon. Keep warm. Heat 1 tbsp oil in a wok over a high heat. Add the chicken and its marinade and stir-fry for 10 minutes. Add the caramel and cook for a few more minutes before adding the toasted sesame seeds. Stir, then arrange in a serving dish. Sprinkle over the remaining sesame seeds and serve immediately with a bowl of fragrant rice.

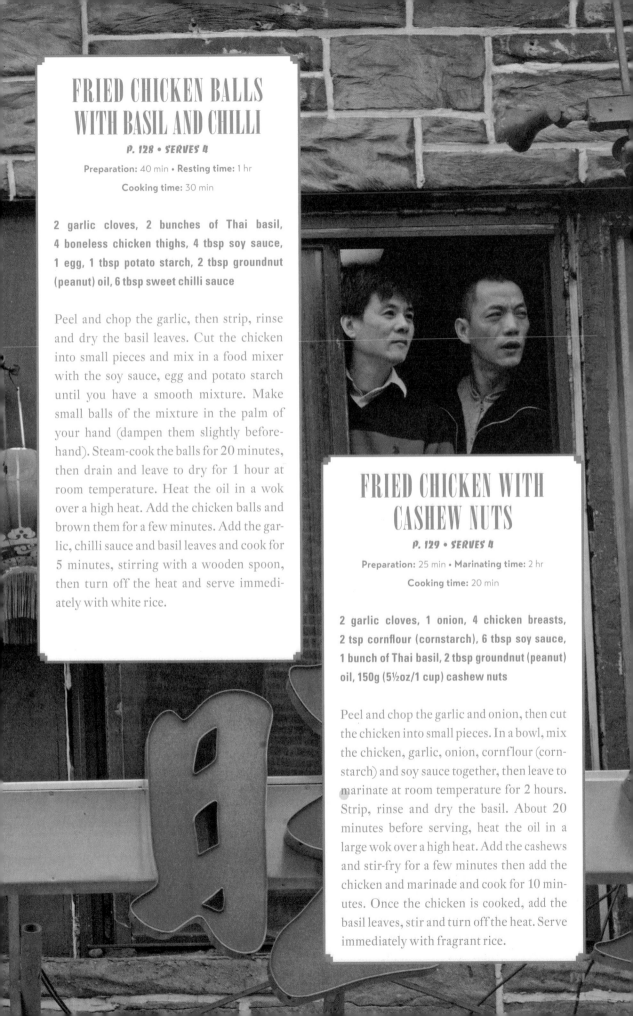

FRIED CHICKEN BALLS WITH BASIL AND CHILLI

P. 128 • SERVES 4

Preparation: 40 min • **Resting time:** 1 hr

Cooking time: 30 min

2 garlic cloves, 2 bunches of Thai basil, 4 boneless chicken thighs, 4 tbsp soy sauce, 1 egg, 1 tbsp potato starch, 2 tbsp groundnut (peanut) oil, 6 tbsp sweet chilli sauce

Peel and chop the garlic, then strip, rinse and dry the basil leaves. Cut the chicken into small pieces and mix in a food mixer with the soy sauce, egg and potato starch until you have a smooth mixture. Make small balls of the mixture in the palm of your hand (dampen them slightly beforehand). Steam-cook the balls for 20 minutes, then drain and leave to dry for 1 hour at room temperature. Heat the oil in a wok over a high heat. Add the chicken balls and brown them for a few minutes. Add the garlic, chilli sauce and basil leaves and cook for 5 minutes, stirring with a wooden spoon, then turn off the heat and serve immediately with white rice.

FRIED CHICKEN WITH CASHEW NUTS

P. 129 • SERVES 4

Preparation: 25 min • **Marinating time:** 2 hr

Cooking time: 20 min

2 garlic cloves, 1 onion, 4 chicken breasts, 2 tsp cornflour (cornstarch), 6 tbsp soy sauce, 1 bunch of Thai basil, 2 tbsp groundnut (peanut) oil, 150g (5½oz/1 cup) cashew nuts

Peel and chop the garlic and onion, then cut the chicken into small pieces. In a bowl, mix the chicken, garlic, onion, cornflour (cornstarch) and soy sauce together, then leave to marinate at room temperature for 2 hours. Strip, rinse and dry the basil. About 20 minutes before serving, heat the oil in a large wok over a high heat. Add the cashews and stir-fry for a few minutes then add the chicken and marinade and cook for 10 minutes. Once the chicken is cooked, add the basil leaves, stir and turn off the heat. Serve immediately with fragrant rice.

BEEF

牛

BEEF

The ox is a sign of the Chinese zodiac and represents strength, calm and happiness. It is also a symbol of agriculture in Chinese civilization, where long ago the animal was used mostly for labour rather than for meat. Traditionally, Asian countries consume very little beef, even though things have begun to change over recent years. Japan is the only Asian country with a strong tradition for its beef industry with the famous *wagyu*, referred to in the West as 'Kobe beef', known for its marbled cuts.

In China, it is unusual for beef to be served rare, and, it is nearly always served in small pieces, either minced (ground) or cut into thin slices. There are, however, a few exceptions, such as Thai beef salad with lemongrass, where the meat is sometimes red, just seared, and *pho* soup, where the beef may sometimes arrive rare but the boiling hot broth soon cooks it through. It is worth noting that in Vietnam you would expect to find only a few pieces of meat per bowl whereas a bowl of *pho* made in the West will be far richer. Other beef dishes include beef on a hot plate, beef with basil, beef in satay sauce and beef spring rolls (known as winter spring rolls in some restaurants to distinguish them from those made with prawns/shrimp). There is also the Vietnamese dish *bo bun*, in which beef is cut into thin strips and marinated.

In China, beef is not butchered in the same way as it is in the West and it is impossible to recognize the various cuts (fillet, tenderloin, sirloin, rump, top round). Over there, beef is simply red meat!

FRIED BEEF WITH BASIL

SERVES 4–6

Preparation: 30 min • **Cooking time:** 20 min

400g (14oz) lean tender beef for frying (sirloin, rump, fillet, tenderloin)

2 red (bell) peppers

1 green (bell) pepper

2 garlic cloves

1 small red chilli

1 bunch of Thai basil

2 tbsp groundnut (peanut) oil

1 tsp caster (superfine) sugar

4 tbsp oyster sauce

6 tbsp soy sauce

Cut the meat into thin slices, then rinse the (bell) peppers, deseed and chop. Peel and chop the garlic, deseed and chop the chilli and strip and rinse the basil leaves.

Heat the oil in a wok and seal the meat in the smoking oil. Leave to brown for a few minutes before adding the sugar, garlic and pepper. Stir-fry for another 5 minutes then add the oyster sauce, soy sauce and chilli and cook for another 2 minutes.

Turn off the heat, add the basil leaves, mix and serve immediately with white rice.

FRIED BEEF
WITH CURRY

P. 144 • SERVES 4

Preparation: 25 min • **Cooking time:** 30 min

400g (14oz) lean tender beef for frying (sirloin, rump, fillet, tenderloin), 1 large onion, 2 garlic cloves, 4 tbsp groundnut (peanut) oil, 2 red chillies, 2 tbsp curry paste, 50ml (2fl oz/scant ¼ cup) beef stock (remains of a beef casserole or a stock cube), 150ml (5fl oz/⅔ cup) coconut milk

Cut the meat into thin slices, then peel the onion and garlic and roughly chop. Heat the oil in a large wok, add the chopped garlic and onion to the hot oil and brown for 1 minute. Add the beef and whole chillies, mix and stir-fry for 1 minute. Add the curry paste then pour in the beef stock and coconut milk and simmer for 25 minutes over a low heat. Turn off the heat, stir and arrange in a shallow dish. Serve with white rice.

'LOT LAC'

P. 145 • SERVES 4–6

Preparation: 25 min • **Marinating time:** 45 min

Cooking time: 15 min

2 tomatoes, 2 onions, 600g (1lb 5oz) lean tender beef for frying (sirloin, rump, fillet, tenderloin), 3 tbsp groundnut (peanut) oil 600g (1lb 5oz/ 3½ cups) cooked rice, 1 bunch of coriander (cilantro)

For the marinade: 4 tbsp nuoc-mâm, 3 garlic cloves, chopped, 2 tbsp caster (superfine) sugar, 1 tsp potato starch, 2 tsp paprika, 3 tbsp groundnut (peanut) oil, 3 tbsp soy sauce, 2 tbsp oyster sauce, 4 tbsp tomato purée, salt and pepper

For the sauce: juice of 3 limes, 2 tbsp nuoc-mâm, 2 tbsp water, 1 tsp caster (superfine) sugar

Prepare the marinade by mixing the nuoc-mâm, garlic, sugar, potato starch, paprika, salt and pepper together. Add the oil, soy sauce, oyster sauce and tomato purée. Slice the tomatoes. Peel and chop the onions. Cut the meat into cubes, toss in the marinade and leave for 45 minutes in a cold place. Combine the sauce ingredients. Heat 1 tbsp oil in a wok. Fry the rice with a little of the marinade to colour it. Keep warm. Wipe the wok clean then fry the chopped onions in the remaining oil until brown. Add the meat with the rest of the marinade and cook for 5 minutes over a high heat. Strip the coriander (cilantro) leaves and rinse. Arrange the rice and the meat on plates. Garnish with the tomato and coriander (cilantro). Serve with the sauce.

'BO BUN'

P. 147 • SERVES 4

Preparation: 40 min • **Marinating time:** 1 hr

Cooking time: 35 min

For the marinade: 1 onion, 1 lemongrass stalk, 500g (1lb 2oz) lean tender beef for frying (sirloin, rump, fillet, tenderloin), 2 tbsp nuoc-mâm, 4 tbsp groundnut (peanut) oil

For the sauce: 2 tbsp nuoc-mâm, 2 tbsp lemon juice, 1 tbsp caster (superfine) sugar, 4 tbsp warm water

For the garnish: 1 bunch of coriander (cilantro), 1 bunch of Thai basil, ½ a lettuce, 1 carrot, 200g (7oz/2 cups) bean sprouts, 1 small cucumber, 6 nems (see p. 34), 200g (7oz) rice vermicelli, 1 tbsp wine vinegar, 2 tbsp peanuts

Peel and chop the onion and lemongrass. Cut the meat into strips and marinate for 1 hour with the onion, lemongrass, nuoc-mâm and groundnut (peanut) oil. Combine the sauce ingredients and set aside. Prepare the garnish. Preheat the oven to 170°C/ 340°F/Gas Mark 3. Rinse, dry and chop the herbs and lettuce. Peel and grate the carrot. Rinse and blanch the bean sprouts, refresh them with cold water and set aside. Rinse, strip and chop the cucumber and set aside. Put the nems in the oven for 20 minutes until brown. Cut them into small pieces and keep warm. Bring a large pan of water to the boil. Drop in the vermicelli, add the vinegar to keep them white and cook for 8–10 minutes, stirring all the time, then rinse under cold water to prevent them sticking. Divide the vermicelli, herbs, carrot and lettuce among four large bowls. Fry the beef and its marinade in a hot wok over a high heat for 5 minutes, or until cooked. Divide the hot meat and nems among the bowls, pour over the nuoc-mâm, sprinkle with the crushed peanuts and serve with the sauce.

AU DÉLICE
DE CONFUCIUS

Paris

As soon as you step through the door you are in China. Ready to sit down to some of the best cooking ever from this huge country? Twenty odd years ago Xue Chaoqing, the restaurant's owner and a cook since the 1970s in China, settled in Paris. 'You will eat dishes here that you won't find anywhere else in Europe', he assures. The food in this restaurant focuses on authenticity and there are no concessions for French taste. Dumplings are the big speciality here, and even the dough is made from wheat flour, typical of North China.

Cuisine and good health go hand in hand for this chef, for whom eating is as much about health as it is pleasure. 'The town where I worked in China before coming to France was the birthplace of Confucius. All the dishes there have a story and a purpose. Sea cucumbers, for example, improve circulation. They are good for women after childbirth.' Among the chef's specialities are sea cucumbers, whelk salad, glazed hock of ham and a remarkable steamed sea bass flavoured with ginger, soy sauce and herbs. This is when we learn that fish is always served at the end of a meal, for the word for fish in Chinese sounds the same as the word meaning 'affluence', so fish symbolises wealth in China. When superstition and the pleasure of food combine...

Opposite: Xue Chaoqing, the owner, arranges the dishes himself during full service.

RAW BEEF
THAI STYLE

P. 154 • SERVES 4–6

Preparation: 25 min

2 bunches of coriander (cilantro), 4 bunches of mint, 1 sweet onion, 2 small red chillies, 3 limes, 2 tsp caster (superfine) sugar, 4 tbsp nuoc-mâm, 60g (2¼oz) minced (ground) beef, 2 tbsp toasted sesame seeds

Rinse, strip and roughly chop the herbs. Peel and chop the sweet onion, then deseed and chop the chillies. Squeeze the limes and mix the juice with the sugar and nuoc-mâm in a large bowl. Add the minced (ground) beef, herbs, onion, chilli and 1½ tbsp of the sesame seeds, mix everything together and arrange on plates. Sprinkle over the remaining ½ tbsp sesame seeds and serve chilled.

FRIED BEEF WITH PEPPER AND SATAY SAUCE

P. 155 • SERVES 6

Preparation: 25 min • **Marinating time:** 30 min

Cooking time: 10 min

700g (1lb 9oz) lean tender beef for frying (sirloin, rump, fillet, tenderloin), 4 tbsp satay sauce, 4 tbsp soy sauce, 2 tbsp nuoc-mâm, 4 tsp caster (superfine) sugar, 1 onion, 1 garlic clove, 1 carrot, ½ a red (bell) pepper, ½ a green (bell) pepper, 1 bunch of coriander (cilantro), 3 tbsp groundnut (peanut)oil

Cut the meat into even strips, then marinate for 30 minutes in a large bowl with the satay sauce, soy sauce, nuoc-mâm and caster (superfine) sugar. Peel and chop the onion and garlic. Peel the carrot and slice it finely using a mandolin. Rinse, deseed and slice the (bell) peppers. Rinse and chop the coriander (cilantro). Heat the groundnut (peanut) oil in a large frying pan. Seal the meat quickly in the hot oil, stir, then add the (bell) peppers, carrot, onion and garlic. Cook over a high heat for 5 minutes, stirring, then turn off the heat, add the coriander (cilantro), mix then serve with white rice.

'BUN BO LUI' BUN CHA BEEF

P. 156 • SERVES 4

Preparation: 25 min • **Marinating time:** 2 hr

Cooking time: 15 min

700g (1lb 9oz) lean tender beef for frying (sirloin, rump, fillet, tenderloin), 200g (7oz) rice vermicelli, 1 tbsp wine vinegar, 1 bunch of coriander (cilantro), 4 spring onion (scallion) stems, 1 tbsp groundnut (peanut) oil, 100g (3½oz/⅔ cup) salted peanuts, crushed
For the marinade: 2 tbsp caster (superfine) sugar, 120ml (4fl oz/½ cup) nuoc-mâm, 1 shallot
For the sauce: 6 tbsp nuoc-mâm, 6 tbsp rice vinegar, 1 garlic clove, peeled and crushed, 3 tbsp caster (superfine) sugar, 12 tbsp warm water

Cut the beef into slices and marinate for 2 hours with the sugar, nuoc-mâm and the peeled and chopped shallot. Bring a large pan of water to the boil. Drop in the vermicelli and add the vinegar. Cook for 8–10 minutes, stirring, then drain and rinse. Rinse, dry and chop the coriander (cilantro) and spring onions (scallions). Combine the sauce ingredients, stirring to dissolve the sugar, then pour into small dishes and set aside. Arrange the vermicelli, coriander (cilantro) and spring onions (scallions) on a large serving plate. Drain the beef and cook in a wok with piping hot oil for 3–4 minutes, then arrange on the vermicelli. Sprinkle with the crushed peanuts and serve with the sauce.

FRIED BEEF WITH ONIONS

SERVES 4

Preparation: 15 min • **Cooking time:** 15 min

400g (14oz) lean tender beef for frying (sirloin, rump, fillet, tenderloin)
1 large carrot
2 large onions

2 garlic cloves
4 tbsp groundnut oil
1 tsp caster (superfine) sugar
3 tbsp soy sauce
2 tbsp satay sauce

1 tbsp oyster sauce
1 tsp potato starch
50ml (2fl oz/scant ¼ cup) beef stock (remains of a beef casserole or use a stock cube)

Cut the meat into thin slices, then peel the carrot and cut into thin slices using a mandolin. Peel the onions and garlic and finely chop.

Heat the oil in a wok and fry the onions, garlic and carrot in the hot oil for 3 minutes. Add the sugar and brown for 5 minutes over a high heat. Add the meat, cook for 2 minutes then deglaze with the soy sauce, satay sauce and oyster sauce and cook for 1 minute.

Stir the potato starch into the hot stock and pour into the wok. Cook for another 5 minutes, then stir and serve with white rice.

FRIED BEEF WITH BROCCOLI

SERVES 4

Preparation: 25 min • **Marinating time:** 4 hr • **Cooking time:** 15 min

---

400g (14oz) lean tender beef
for frying (sirloin, rump,
fillet, tenderloin)
2 garlic cloves
20g (¾oz) piece ginger

3 tbsp light soy sauce
(+ 3 tbsp for cooking)
4 tbsp oyster sauce
1 tsp five-spice mixture
250g (9oz) broccoli

2 tsp cornflour (cornstarch)
100ml (3½fl oz/scant ½ cup) beef
stock (remains of a beef
casserole or use a stock cube)
2 tbsp groundnut (peanut) oil

Cut the beef into thin slices. Peel the garlic and ginger, then chop the garlic and grate the ginger. In a bowl, mix the beef with the 3 tbsp soy sauce, oyster sauce, five-spice, garlic and ginger. Cover with clingfilm (plastic wrap) and leave to marinate for 4 hours in the refrigerator.

Chop the broccoli into small pieces, then whisk the cornflour (cornstarch) into the warm stock and set aside.

About 10 minutes before serving, heat the oil in a wok over a high heat and fry the broccoli for 1 minute. Remove and set aside.

Pour the beef and marinade into the wok and stir-fry for 1 minute over a high heat, then add the stock, the remaining soy sauce and the broccoli. Mix and cook for a few minutes until the sauce has thickened and coated all the ingredients. Serve immediately.

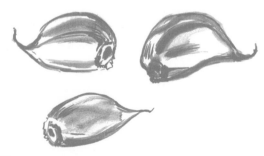

PORK

The consumption of pork is increasing all the time in Asia, and the Chinese account for more than half of the total pork consumed worldwide. In fact, three quarters of the meat eaten in China is pork: it is very much a favourite product. The meat is suitable for many types of cooking – it can be glazed, cooked in a sweet-and-sour sauce, boiled, grilled or roasted – which is clearly one of the reasons for its great success in Asian cuisine.

PORK

A lot of pork is eaten in Asia. It is prepared with all kinds of sauces and for all types of cooking: fried, boiled, with sauce, in a casserole, stir-fried or glazed. Tripe is also much appreciated: it is boiled and finely chopped in Vietnam, but also marinated and fried in China, which makes it crispy on the outside, soft on the inside, and a reddish colour from the marinade. Western restaurants usually use a ready-made mix for this: *char siu* sauce, made principally from soy sauce with added spices, sugar, etc.

Sweet-and-sour pork is extremely popular in the West. But it has become so ubiquitous, and is sometimes so badly cooked, that it is easy to forget the truly sublime and classic dish it originally was. The pieces of pork should be lightly fried, then thickly coated with sweet-and-sour sauce and garnished with crunchy pieces of pepper and flash-fried fresh pineapple chunks. It is the ultimate dish that everyone should get to try once in a lifetime. But you need the right address!

In Asian recipes, pork is nearly always chopped into small pieces, but the restaurant Au délice de Confucius in Paris (see p. 150) offers a dish that is quite unusual, if not unique in France. It's a pork hock cooked whole like a 'confit' and coated with a thick sauce. In Vietnam and in numerous restaurants in the capital you can eat *bun cha*, grilled pork belly served with meatballs, rice vermicelli and plenty of fresh herbs, as is typical in Vietnamese cuisine. You roll the meat, the vermicelli and the herbs in a lettuce leaf yourself – fresh and healthy eating!

HOW TO EAT WITH CHOPSTICKS...

Newcomers are sometimes a little wary of chopsticks, afraid that they'll be unable to handle them and will spill food all over the table. However, it is surprisingly easy to learn how to use them, and definitely worth persevering, because Chinese food just tastes better eaten this way! Chopsticks are used all over Asia, except in Thailand, where a spoon and fork is more usual. However, many Thai restaurants in the West will still put chopsticks on the table, as their customers expect to eat Asian food with them.

Just as in the West we have a tradition of fine tableware with silver cutlery, so there are also top-quality chopsticks made of ivory or fine wood. You do not hold and use chopsticks any old how: for example, you should never stick your chopsticks into a bowl of rice or noodles, which is a death omen and, in fact, how chopsticks are presented at funerals.

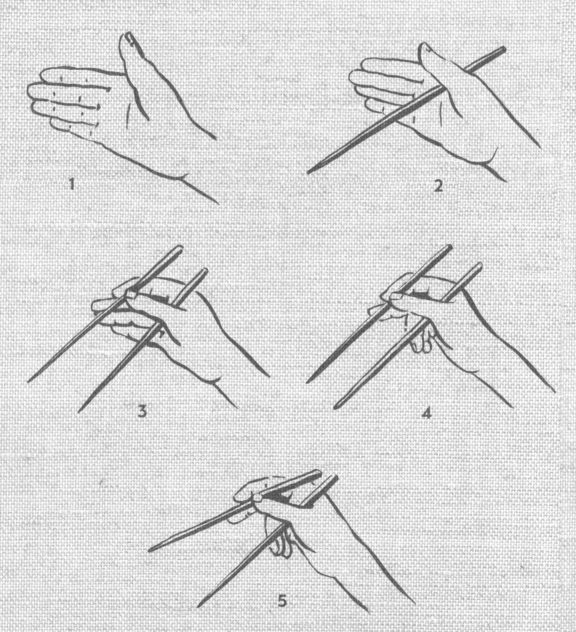

...AND WHAT YOU SHOULD NEVER DO WITH CHOPSTICKS

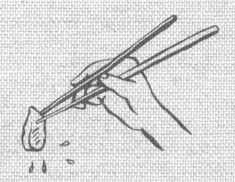

Drain the sauce from a piece of food picked up with chopsticks

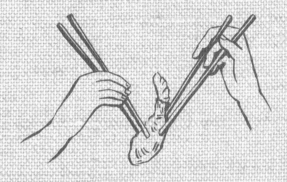

Pass a piece of food from one guest to another with chopsticks

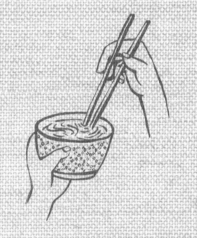

Mix your soup with chopsticks

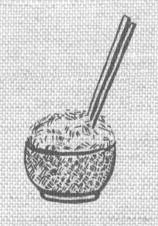

Stick chopsticks into a bowl of rice

Pierce a piece of food with chopsticks

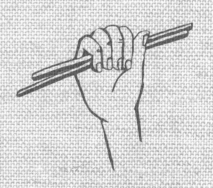

Threaten another guest with your chopsticks

CANTONESE PORK SPARE RIBS

SERVES 4-6

Preparation: 30 min • **Marinating time:** 4 hr • **Cooking time:** 50 min

4 garlic cloves

2 green (bell) peppers

1.5kg (3 lb) pork spare ribs

4 tbsp runny honey

250ml (9fl oz/generous 1 cup) rice wine

2 tbsp rice vinegar

8 tbsp soy sauce

1 tbsp caster (superfine) sugar

1 tbsp groundnut (peanut) oil

Peel and chop the garlic, then deseed and chop the (bell) peppers. Remove some of the fat from the spare ribs, cut into pieces and marinate for 4 hours at room temperature (not too warm a place) with the honey, wine, vinegar, soy sauce, sugar and garlic.

Preheat the oven to 210°C/410°F/Gas Mark 6½. Drain the spare ribs and arrange on a grill (broiler) rack set over a roasting tin with a little water in the bottom of the tin. Cook in the oven for 40 minutes, turning them from time to time so that they brown evenly. Drain on a plate.

Heat the oil in a wok and fry the peppers for 1 minute. Add the spare ribs and marinade, then let them caramelize and the sauce thicken for 5–8 minutes over a high heat. Serve the spare ribs with white rice.

SWEET-AND-SOUR PORK WITH BASIL

SERVES 6

Preparation: 35 min • **Marinating time:** 1 hr • **Cooking time:** 25 min

---

500g (1lb 2oz) rack of pork
or pork shoulder
9 tbsp soy sauce
1 bunch of Thai basil
1 large onion

1 x 250g (9oz) can pineapple
in syrup
1 tbsp groundnut (peanut) oil
2 tbsp cornflour (cornstarch)
4 tbsp oyster sauce

3 tbsp rice vinegar
2 tbsp ketchup
300g (10½oz/scant 2½ cups)
flour
cooking oil

Cut the pork into thin slices, toss in 5 tbsp of the soy sauce then cover and marinate for 1 hour. Rinse, dry and strip the basil, then peel and finely chop the onion. Drain the pineapple rings, reserving the syrup, and cut into small pieces.

Heat the groundnut (peanut) oil in a wok, then fry the pineapple and onion quickly. Once they are browned, add the cornflour (cornstarch). Mix, then whisk in the pineapple syrup, the remaining soy sauce, the oyster sauce, vinegar and ketchup and stir-fry for 25 minutes. Turn off the heat and set aside.

Prepare and heat a deep-fryer then add the basil to the hot oil and quickly deep-fry. Remove with a slotted spoon and drain on a plate.

Drain the pork pieces, dip them in the flour, then carefully lower them into the deep-fryer and fry for 5–8 minutes, shaking well until they are cooked and golden. Drain on kitchen paper (paper towels) then add to the wok with the sauce. Mix, and arrange everything in a large dish. Cover with the basil leaves and serve with white rice.

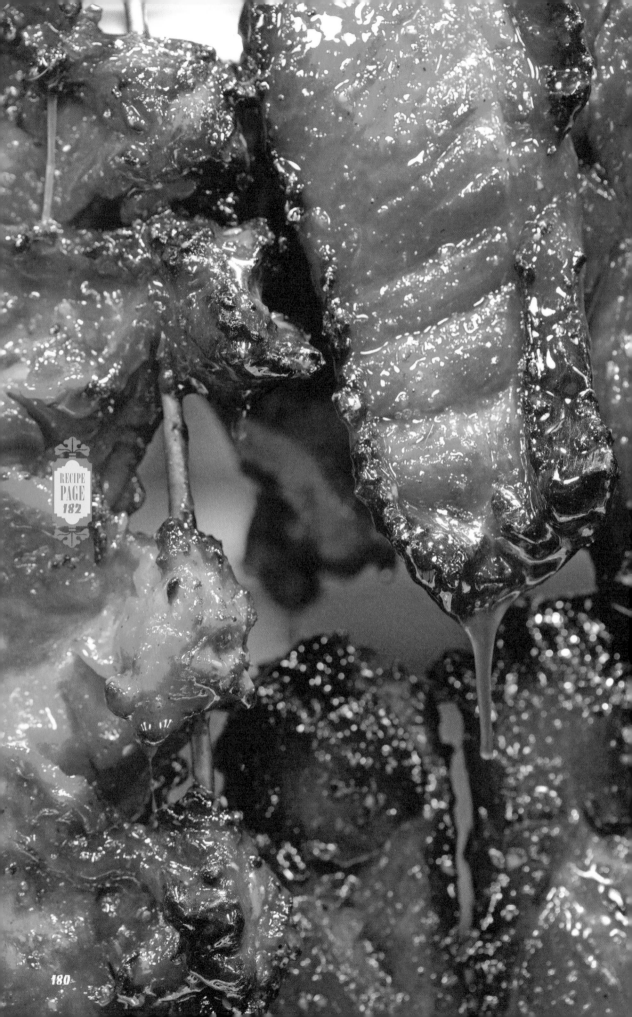

GRILLED PORK CHOPS WITH LEMONGRASS

P. 179 • SERVES 4

Preparation: 20 min • **Marinating time:** 12 hr

Cooking time: 15 min

2 shallots, 1 garlic clove, 1 bunch of coriander (cilantro), 4 lemongrass stalks, 2 tbsp nuoc-mâm, 6 tbsp soy sauce, 2 tsp caster (superfine) sugar, 1 tsp five-spice mixture, 4 pork chops on the bone, 2 tbsp groundnut (peanut) oil, a few rings of canned pineapple in syrup

Peel and finely chop the shallots and garlic. Rinse the coriander (cilantro), then snip off the stalks and keep the leaves. Chop the lemongrass in a food mixer. Mix all these ingredients together with the nuoc-mâm, soy sauce, sugar and five-spice in a large dish. Add the pork chops, turn to coat and leave to marinate overnight in a cold place. Heat the oil in a large frying pan. Seal the pork chops, then cook for 10 minutes, turning from time. Reduce the heat, pour in the marinade and cook for 5 minutes, basting the chops regularly with the sauce to glaze them, until all the sauce is used. Arrange the chops on a serving plate, garnish with the pineapple rings, sprinkle over the coriander (cilantro) leaves and serve with rice.

CARAMELIZED PORK

P. 180 • SERVES 4–6

Preparation: 15 min • **Cooking time:** 1 hr

2 pork spare ribs, 250g (9oz) sugar cubes, 100ml (3½fl oz/scant ½ cup) light soy sauce

Preheat the oven to 170°C/340°F/Gas Mark 3. Cut the ribs into large pieces , arrange them on a grill (broiler) rack set over a roasting tin and cook in the oven for 1 hour. Place the sugar in a large pan, pour in a small glass of water and cook for 3–4 minutes, watching all the time, until you have a light caramel. Pour the soy sauce over the hot caramel and stir with a wooden spoon until mixed. Add the ribs to the caramel and cook for 2 minutes, stirring all the time to make sure the ribs are coated with the caramel. Serve piping hot with a bowl of fragrant white rice.

HANOI 'BUN CHA'

P. 181 • SERVES 4–6

Preparation: 25 min • **Marinating time:** 2 hr

Cooking time: 20 min

800g (1lb 12oz) pork belly or shoulder, 2 tbsp caster (superfine) sugar, 1 shallot, 120ml (4fl oz/ ½ cup) nuoc-mâm, 150g (5½oz) rice vermicelli, 1 tbsp wine vinegar, 200g (7oz) green papaya, 1 batavia lettuce, 1 bunch of coriander (cilantro), 1 bunch of Thai basil, 1 bunch of flat-leaf parsley

For the sauce: 6 tbsp nuoc-mâm, 6 tbsp rice vinegar, 1 garlic clove, crushed, 1 small chilli, deseeded and finely chopped, 3 tbsp caster (superfine) sugar, 12 tbsp warm water

Cut the pork into small pieces, then marinate for 2 hours with the sugar, chopped shallot and nuoc-mâm, stirring occasionally. Bring a pan of water to the boil, add the rice vermicelli and vinegar and cook, stirring, for 8–10 minutes, then drain and rinse. Peel the papaya and cut into thin strips using a mandolin. Rinse the lettuce and herbs. Prepare the sauce by mixing everything together until the sugar dissolves. Divide the sauce among bowls and add the papaya. Arrange the herbs, vermicelli and salad in a large dish on the table. Drain the pork and grill on the barbecue for 15 minutes or 5 minutes in an oven preheated to 200°C/400°F/Gas Mark 6 until cooked and golden brown. Divide among the bowls and serve with the side dishes.

Make the same dish using minced (ground) pork marinated, then formed into small balls.

PORK BELLY
WITH CHESTNUTS

SERVES 4

Preparation: 25 min • **Cooking time:** 1 hr 30 min • **Resting time:** 2 hr

1kg (2¼lb) pork belly

1 tbsp five-spice mixture

1 garlic clove

50g (1¾oz) piece ginger

2 tbsp groundnut (peanut) oil

2 tbsp brown sugar

100ml (3½fl oz/scant ½ cup)
Chinese rice wine

6 tbsp soy sauce

400g (14oz) jar of chestnuts

Preheat the oven to 170°C/340°F/Gas Mark 3. Rub the meat with the five-spice, place it on a grill (broiler) rack set over a roasting tin and cook in the oven for 1 hour. Turn off the oven and leave the pork to cool in the oven for at least 2 hours (or overnight).

Peel and crush the garlic, then peel and grate the ginger. About 30 minutes before serving, cut the meat into large cubes.

Heat the oil in a casserole (Dutch oven) over a high heat, add the pork and fry for a few minutes until browned. Reduce the heat and add the sugar, crushed garlic and grated ginger and let it caramelize, stirring constantly.

Deglaze the casserole (Dutch oven) with the rice wine then let it reduce by half. Pour in the soy sauce and reduce again, coating the meat with sauce to glaze it. Add the chestnuts and heat for 5 minutes, stirring carefully, then serve.

SOUP WITH GLAZED PORK, NOODLES AND DUMPLINGS

SERVES 6–8

Preparation: 1 hr • **Cooking time:** 15 min

1 litre (1¾ pints/4 cups)
chicken stock
1 pak choi
400g (14oz) roast pork
200g (7oz) Chinese egg noodles
4 spring onion (scallion) stems

For the dumplings:
1 garlic clove
300g (10½oz) lean pork
100g (3½oz) peeled prawns
(shrimp)
1 tbsp soy sauce

1 tsp sesame oil
1 tsp cane sugar
1 egg yolk
24 wonton pastry squares

Prepare the dumplings. Peel and finely chop the garlic. Chop the pork and prawns (shrimp) in a food mixer, then add the garlic, soy sauce, sesame oil and sugar. Use your hands to mix all the ingredients together well. Beat the egg yolk in a bowl with 2 tbsp cold water and set aside.

Baste one wonton pastry square with the egg yolk. Place a knob of the filling in the centre of the pastry square and close up the dumpling like a little purse. Continue until you have used up all the mixture. Drop the dumplings into a large pan of salted boiling water and cook for 8 minutes, then divide among six large bowls.

Bring the chicken stock to the boil in a pan. Cut the pak choi into six lengthways then cook it for about 5–6 minutes in the chicken stock. Chop the roast pork and set aside.

Cook the noodles in boiling water according to the packet instructions, then drain and divide among the bowls. Add the pieces of roast pork and cabbage, then pour over the piping hot stock and sprinkle with chopped spring onion (scallion) before serving.

DONG HUANG

Paris

There is such a thing as a quality, straightforward, inexpensive Vietnamese restaurant with food prepared by real Vietnamese cooks! Forget the deco and the niceties of service: cutlery and chopsticks are placed in a bowl on the table – you serve yourself. The same goes for the sauces, which are passed round from table to table. As soon as you order, the dishes arrive promptly at the table, and when it's time to clear, they are simply piled up. There are no frills; it's all about taste: the flavours are fresh and everything is homemade. A product of the Indochinese immigration, this restaurant opened in the 1980s. The menu is 100% Vietnamese: *bo bun*, variations of *pho* with tripe, meatballs, with a satay or prawn (shrimp) broth, *bun cha*, *banh cuon*, not forgetting the specialities of North Vietnam, such as salad with papaya, bacon and prawns (shrimp) or soup with prawns (shrimp) and shredded crab, and service is non-stop. You step out of this restaurant with a smile on your face, your taste buds refreshed, your stomach satisfied and your wallet not too much thinner than when you entered!

Opposite: The young owner and his cousin, the chef, pose in the restaurant kitchen amidst steaming pots of broth.

RECIPE
PAGE
197

'NEM NUONG'
GRILLED PORK BALLS

P. 193 • SERVES 4

Preparation: 45 min • **Cooking time:** 25 min

3 garlic cloves, 1.2kg (2lb 12oz) pork shoulder,
1 tbsp roasted rice flour, 1 tbsp potato starch,
1 tbsp yeast, 3 tbsp water, 2 tbsp brown sugar,
½ tsp salt, 2 tbsp nuoc-mâm, cooking oil
For the garnish: 100g (3½oz) rice vermicelli,
1 tbsp wine vinegar, 1 bunch of coriander
(cilantro), 1 bunch of mint, a few lettuce leaves,
2 small cucumbers, 50g (1¾oz) peanuts

First make the garnish. Bring a pan of water
to the boil, drop in the vermicelli, add the
vinegar and cook for 8–10 minutes, stirring
constantly, then rinse under cold water.
Rinse and dry the herbs and lettuce leaves.
Rinse the cucumbers and cut into small
sticks, leaving the skin on. Crush the peanuts in a mortar and pestle. Peel and crush
the garlic. Cut the meat into pieces and put
it through a food mixer. Place it in a bowl
and use your hands to mix it well with the
flour, potato starch, garlic, yeast, water,
sugar, salt and nuoc-nâm. Oil your hands
then form the mixture into small balls. It's
important to knead each ball 20–30 times
to make sure it doesn't fall apart as it cooks.
Spike four pork balls with each skewer then
grill on the barbecue for 15 minutes or in a
moderate oven until cooked through. Serve
sprinkled with peanuts, herbs, lettuce, vermicelli and a dipping sauce. Alternatively,
serve these balls wrapped in rice sheets
with vermicelli and herbs, like a spring roll.

'TONKATSU'

P. 194 • SERVES 4

Preparation: 30 min • **Cooking time:** 10 min

4 boneless pork chops or cutlets, 2 eggs, 300g (10½oz/4 cups) panko (Japanese breadcrumbs), 200g (7oz/generous 1½ cups) flour, cooking oil, 'special tonkatsu' sauce or sweet-and-sour chilli sauce, salt and pepper

Flatten the pork with a rolling pin (between two pieces of clingfilm/plastic wrap). Beat the egg in a dish, pour the breadcrumbs in another and the flour in a third. Dip the pork in the flour, then in the beaten egg and then in the breadcrumbs. Chill in the refrigerator for 10 minutes. Prepare and heat a deep-fryer then carefully lower the breaded pork, two pieces at a time, into the hot oil and fry until golden. Drain on kitchen paper (paper towels), then cut into thin slices about 2cm (¾ inch) thick. Serve hot with the sauce.

SHREDDED PORK WITH BAMBOO SHOOTS

P. 195 • SERVES 4–6

Preparation: 35 min • **Marinating time:** 3 hr

Cooking time: 25 min

3 garlic cloves, 1 small can of bamboo shoots, 1 pork fillet (tenderloin), 3 tsp caster (superfine) sugar, 4 tbsp soy sauce, 2 tsp or rice vinegar, 4 tbsp groundnut (peanut) oil, green leaves of 1 leek

Peel and chop the garlic. Drain, then chop the bamboo shoots, then remove the fat from the pork fillet (tenderloin) and cut into small strips. Mix the pork, garlic, sugar, soy sauce, vinegar and bamboo shoots in a bowl, cover and leave to marinate at room temperature for 3 hours. When ready to serve, heat the oil in a wok over a high heat and sear the meat with its marinade. Cook for 5 minutes, stirring constantly until reduced and caramelized. Arrange everything in a dish, sprinkle with the finely chopped raw leek and serve with a bowl of white rice.

DUCK

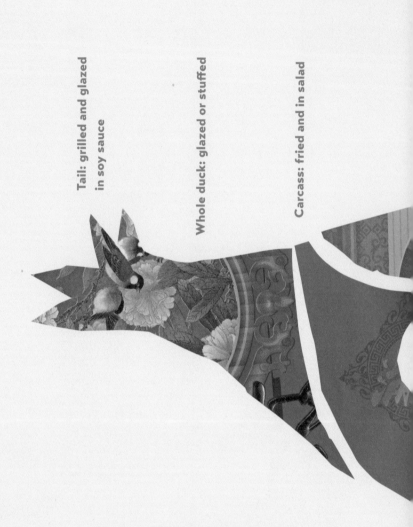

Tail: grilled and glazed in soy sauce

Whole duck: glazed or stuffed

Carcass: fried and in salad

EVERY PART OF THE DUCK IS EDIBLE

In the West, we distinguish between two different types of Peking duck. Restaurants of a certain standard serve the real two- or three-course Peking duck (see p. 214), whereas the more common establishments hang whole roasted ducks, flavoured with five-spice in their window, then at the customer's request they are quartered and cut into pieces. These are typical of South China and can be served with noodles, in a soup or in a bowl of plain rice. These ducks, raised in the West, are quite fatty, their skin is a deep reddish brown after having been cooked and their meat is soft and tender.

Every part of the duck is edible in Asia: not only its meat and skin, but also its webbed feet – you have to suck the skin between the small bones – and even its tongue, which is generally served stir-fried with salt and pepper or braised in the beak.

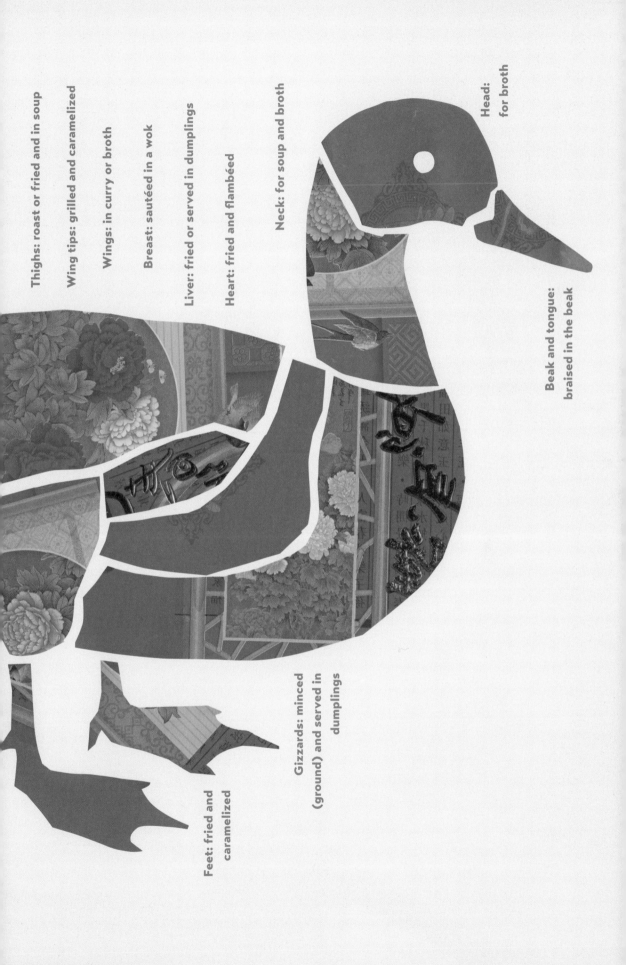

Thighs: roast or fried and in soup

Wing tips: grilled and caramelized

Wings: in curry or broth

Breast: sautéed in a wok

Liver: fried or served in dumplings

Heart: fried and flambéed

Neck: for soup and broth

Head: for broth

Beak and tongue: braised in the beak

Feet: fried and caramelized

Gizzards: minced (ground) and served in dumplings

PEKING DUCK

Peking duck is more than a recipe, it is an art of cooking and eating, a temple of Chinese gastronomy, in the same way that *pâté en croûte* (meat pie) or Beef Wellington are stalwart dishes of French and English cuisine. As the name suggests, Peking duck is a speciality from Beijing and certain extremely renowned restaurants serve only this dish.

The quality of the produce is of paramount importance, but the preparation is just as crucial. The ducks are on average three months old at the time they are killed, in order to guarantee the tenderness of the meat. Air is injected between the duck's skin and its meat and the animal is then scalded in water and sprayed several times with sugared water mixed with vinegar. Some restaurants prepare a mix of spices (liquorice, star anise, cinnamon, black cardamom, fennel) that also flavours the skin. Finally, the animal is air-dried for between six hours and two days, then placed in a cold room for several hours before being cooked in the oven for 45–75 minutes depending on the recipe. Traditionally, an oven heated with peach wood is used for the cooking.

The duck, now glazed, is then presented in several courses. On a trolley placed next to the clients' table, the chef carefully removes strips of skin without the meat, which are eaten rolled up in rice pancakes, served with hoisin sauce and chives or spring onion (scallion) stems. The meat is then chopped into small pieces and served sautéed with vegetables, and finally, the broth is served at the end of the meal.

The quality of a Peking duck is determined by the crispiness of its skin and the tenderness of its meat, but the thinness of the rice pancake that accompanies this exceptional dish is also an important factor.

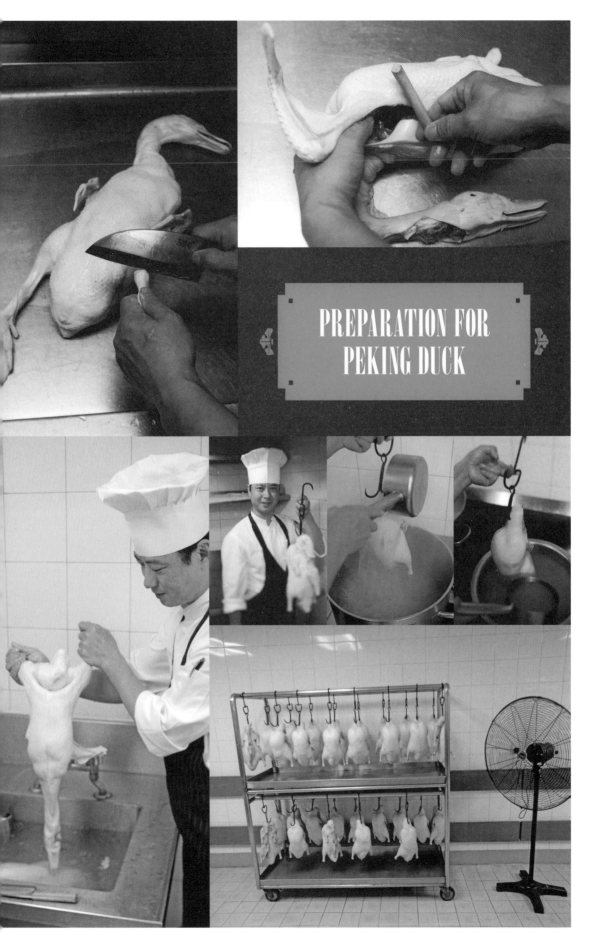

PREPARATION FOR PEKING DUCK

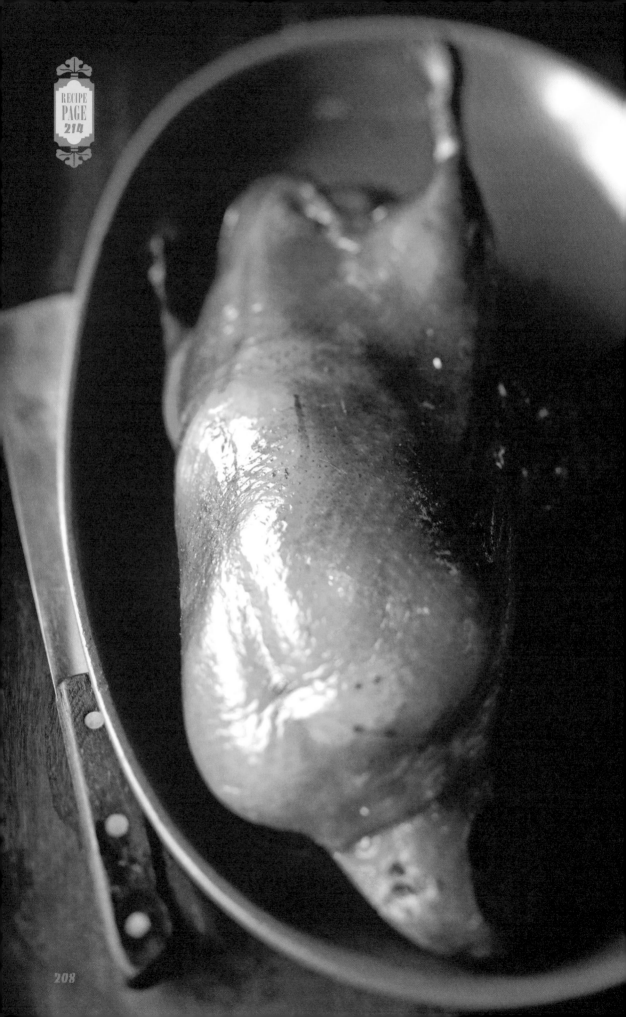

GLAZED PEKING DUCK TO MAKE AT HOME

P. 208 • SERVES 4

Preparation: 3 hr • Drying time: 7–8 hr

Cooking time: 1 hr 35 min

1 large meaty duck (about 2.5kg/5½lb when drawn), 5 tbsp liquid honey (or molasses), 120ml (4fl oz/½ cup) boiling water, 8 small spring onions (scallions)
For the syrup: 250ml (9fl oz/generous 1 cup) sweet soy paste (or hoisin sauce), 50g (1¾oz) piece ginger, 1 small chilli, a few spoonfuls of light soy sauce

Wash the duck under cold running water and remove any small bumps from the skin. (For those who want to try the authentic recipe, carefully empty out the duck via its neck and place a bamboo stick inside crossways to widen the ribcage. Blow into it or use a small pump to inflate the duck and then close the opening). Dry the duck with a clean cloth then hang the duck in an airy place and let it dry for 5–6 hours (3 hours if you put a fan over it to speed up the drying). Mix the honey with the boiling water in a large pan. Place the duck in a basin and pour boiling water over it 2–3 times. Drain the duck, dry it again, then place it on a covered grill (broiler) rack with the basin underneath. Baste the whole duck with the honey syrup, then dry for 1 hour. Repeat until there is no syrup left. While it is drying for a final time, preheat the oven to 200°C/400°F/Gas Mark 6. Place the duck in a roasting tin then put into the oven for 45 minutes. Keep a close eye to make sure it doesn't burn; if necessary reduce the temperature to 180°C/350°F/Gas Mark 4. Turn the duck over and cook for 50 minutes. Increase the temperature to 250°C/410°F/Gas Mark 9 for the last 5–10 minutes so that it turns golden and the skin becomes crispy.

FIRST DUCK SERVING

THE SKIN

P. 210

Present your guests with the whole duck, then, using a sharp knife, cut away just the crispy skin from the surface and arrange it fanned out on a small plate. Serve this rolled up in little pancakes (see the recipe below or purchase in Asian stores), garnished with cucumber sticks and spring onions (scallions), and seasoned with hoisin sauce or sweet soy paste mixed with a little soy sauce.

SECOND DUCK SERVING

THE MEAT

P. 212

Having served the skin, remove the meat from the duck carcass, roughly chop it and fry it quickly in a wok with a little soy sauce, grated ginger and finely chopped chilli.

THIRD DUCK SERVING

THE CARCASS

P. 209

Break up the carcass and fry it briefly in a casserole (Dutch oven) with half a finely chopped Chinese cabbage. Cover with water and leave to simmer over a low heat for 30 minutes, then add 2 tbsp light soy sauce. Serve piping hot in small bowls.

PANCAKES

P. 212–213 • SERVES 4

185g (6½oz/1½ cups) wheat flour, 125ml (4fl oz/½ cup) boiling water, sesame seed oil

Sift the flour into a large bowl, make a little well in the centre, then pour in the boiling water and mix carefully with a wooden spoon. Knead until it has cooled and you have a smooth dough. Cover with clingfilm (plastic wrap) and set aside to rest in a warm place for 25 minutes.

Make a long roll of dough and cut it into 20 even pieces. Flatten each piece in the palm of your hand, then roll out into small thin pancakes with a rolling pin. Baste with sesame oil and set aside without stacking them so that they don't stick to each other.

Heat a large pan (preferably one with a heavy base), wipe with sesame oil using a piece of kitchen paper (paper towel) and cook the pancakes on each side until small brown spots start to form.

CHEZ VONG

Paris

Where does Mr Vong come from? How did he start cooking? What are his passions? The mute chef does not reply. He cooks his beautiful dishes decorated with sculpted vegetables in silence, leaving his wife to act as his spokesperson. Born in Macao, his mother was an excellent cook, but it must not be said out loud. The man is passionate about kung fu and acupuncture, but hush! Mrs Vong doesn't understand why her husband is so discreet about such innocent questions, but he's probably just extremely modest.

After a stay in Hong Kong, Mr Vong arrived in France 40 years ago and his establishment soon became the most sought-after Asian restaurant in Paris. In the 1980s, actors, producers and politicians flocked to his table to savour exquisite Chinese cuisine from Canton. The 'secret' behind Mr Vong's famous three-course Peking duck is Chinese cuisine made with top-quality French produce. On the menu is poultry from Bresse, duck from Challans and beef that is not 'overcooked', he specifies. The sizzling prawns (shrimp) on a hotplate, the glazed Bresse chicken and the scallops with their five different flavours are all classics. Here is a great chef in the proper sense of the word.

Opposite: Chez Vong is one of the oldest Chinese restaurants in Paris and specializes in three-course Peking duck.

FRIED DUCK WITH PINEAPPLE

SERVES 6

Preparation: 35 min • **Marinating time:** 1 hr • **Cooking time:** 25 min

1 x 250g (9oz) can pineapple in syrup	2 duck thighs and 2 duck breasts	2 tbsp oyster sauce
2 garlic cloves	6 tbsp soy sauce	1 green (bell) pepper
1 large onion	2 tbsp white rice vinegar	1 red (bell) pepper
50g (1¾oz) piece ginger	2 tbsp ketchup	1 tbsp sunflower oil
	2 tsp cornflour (cornstarch)	

Drain the pineapple slices, reserving half the syrup, and cut the pineapple into pieces. Peel and chop the garlic and onion, then peel and grate the ginger.

Bone the duck thighs. Remove the fat from the duck breasts and thighs, then chop into pieces. In a bowl, mix the duck, soy sauce, garlic, onion and ginger, then cover and marinate for 1 hour in the refrigerator.

Bring the pineapple syrup, vinegar, ketchup, cornflour (cornstarch) and oyster sauce to the boil in a small pan, then strain and set aside. If the sauce is too thick add a little water. Trim the (bell) peppers and deseed, then cut into slices.

Heat the oil in a large wok and fry the duck with the marinade. Let it brown for a few minutes then add the (bell) peppers and cook for 5 minutes over a high heat, stirring constantly. Pour in the sauce, mix and cook for another 2 minutes. Turn off the heat and serve immediately with rice.

FRIED DUCK WITH BAMBOO SHOOTS

P. 227 • SERVES 6

Preparation: 35 min • **Marinating time:** 1 hr

Cooking time: 25 min

2 garlic cloves, 1 large onion, 5 dried black mushrooms, 50g (1¾oz) piece ginger, 2 duck thighs and 2 duck breasts, 5 tbsp soy sauce, 1 tbsp sesame oil, 1 small can of bamboo shoots, 2 tbsp groundnut (peanut) oil, 4 tbsp oyster sauce

Peel and chop the garlic and onion. Soak the mushrooms in a bowl of warm water for 15 minutes until soft. Peel and grate the ginger. Bone the duck thighs. Remove the fat from the thighs and breasts then chop into pieces. In a bowl, mix the duck with the garlic, onion, ginger, soy sauce and sesame oil. Leave to marinate for 1 hour in a cold place. Drain and rinse the bamboo shoots. Drain, squeeze and chop the mushrooms. Heat the groundnut (peanut) oil in a large wok over a high heat and fry the duck and marinade. Let it brown for a few minutes then add the mushrooms, bamboo shoots, oyster sauce and a little water. Reduce the heat and cook for 10 minutes stirring regularly. Serve immediately with white rice.

DUCK RICE

P. 228 • SERVES 4–6

Preparation: 35 min • **Drying time:** 5–6 hr

Cooking time: 1 hr 45 min

1 Barbary duck, 2 tbsp salt, 1 tbsp caster (super-fine) sugar, 50ml (2fl oz/scant ¼ cup) dark soy sauce, 2 tablespoons light soy sauce, 4 star anise, 4 garlic cloves, 1½ tablespoons rice vinegar, 3 lemongrass stalks, 100g (3½oz) piece galangal, 3 cloves, 2 cinnamon sticks, 1 tsp black peppercorns

Season the duck inside and out with the salt and sugar. Heat a large wok without any oil then brown the duck on all sides. Add the soy sauces, star anise, crushed garlic, vinegar, chopped lemongrass, roughly chopped galangal, cloves, cinnamon sticks and peppercorns. Bring to the boil, basting the duck regularly. Add 100ml (3½ fl oz/scant ½ cup) water and cook for 20 minutes over a low heat, basting all the time. Turn the duck and cook for another hour, still over a low heat, basting regularly to glaze it. If the sauce reduces too quickly, add a little water. When the duck is cooked, drain and leave it to dry at room temperature (you can hang it in an airy place) for 5–6 hours (3 hours if you put a fan over it). Let the sauce reduce slightly. Check the seasoning and strain. When you are ready to eat, reheat the duck in the oven, then cut it into pieces and serve with the sauce and white rice. You can also add a little dried chilli, if you like.

FRIED DUCK WITH VEGETABLES AND CRISPY NOODLES

P. 229 • SERVES 4

Preparation: 1 hr • **Marinating time:** 1 hr

Cooking time: 1 hr

5 black mushrooms, 2 garlic cloves, 1 large onion, 50g (1¾oz) piece ginger, 2 duck thighs and 2 duck breasts, 6 tbsp soy sauce, 200g (7oz) Chinese egg noodles, 4 tbsp sunflower oil, 1 carrot, ¼ of a cabbage, 2 courgettes (zucchini), 300g (10½oz) broccoli, 2 tbsp oyster sauce, cooking oil, salt and pepper

Soak the mushrooms in a bowl of warm water for 15 minutes until soft. Peel and chop the garlic and onion, then peel and grate the ginger. Bone the duck thighs. Remove the fat from the thighs and breasts then chop into pieces. In a bowl, mix the duck, soy sauce, garlic, onion and ginger together, cover and leave to marinate for 1 hour in a cool place. Drop the noodles into a bowl of cold water for 30 minutes, just long enough to separate them. Drain and mix them with 2 tbsp oil. Drain and squeeze out the mushrooms, then chop them. Rinse the other vegetables. Chop the carrot, cabbage and courgettes (zucchini) and cut the broccoli into small pieces. Prepare and heat a deep-fryer and cook the noodles in two batches. Leave them to brown for a few minutes, then drain on kitchen paper (paper towels) and keep warm. Heat the rest of the oil in a wok. Fry the duck and marinade for a few minutes until brown, then add the vegetables, mushrooms and oyster sauce and stir-fry until almost all the liquid has evaporated. Season and remove from the heat. Divide the noodles among the plates, add the duck and vegetables and serve immediately.

FIVE-SPICE ROAST DUCK

SERVES 4

Preparation: 30 min • Marinating time: 2 hr • Cooking time: 1 hr

1 Barbary duck

2 tbsp five-spice mixture

(+ a little extra to serve)

1 garlic clove

½ tsp ground cumin

2 tbsp runny honey

5 tbsp soy sauce

juice of 1 lemon

a few coriander (cilantro)

sprigs

salt and pepper

Baste the inside and outside of the duck with 1 tbsp of the five-spice mixture, then season with salt and pepper and set aside.

Peel and crush the garlic. Put it in a mortar with the remaining five-spice and the cumin and grind to a smooth paste with the pestle, then add the honey and soy sauce. Prick the duck all over with a fork then baste it all over with the five-spice and honey mixture. Leave to marinate and dry for 2 hours at room temperature.

Preheat the oven to 160°C/325°F/Gas Mark 2–3. Place the duck in a large dish and cook in the oven for 1 hour, basting it regularly with the spice mixture. The duck should be very well cooked, tender and caramel coloured.

Cut the duck into pieces and serve with the lime juice, a few coriander (cilantro) leaves, a little more five-spice mixture and white rice.

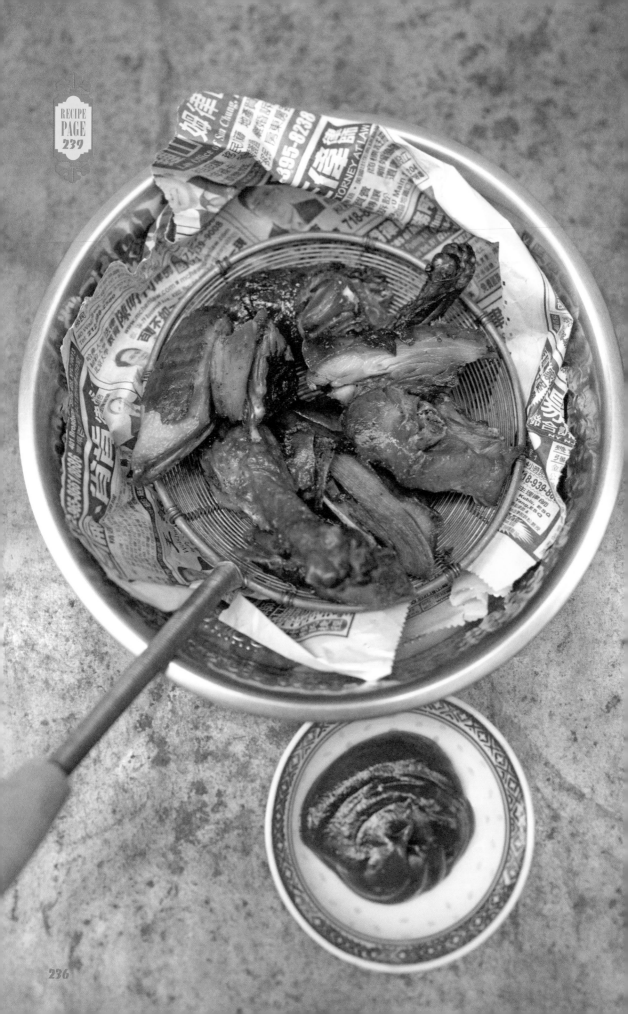

FRIED DUCK WITH FRESH PEPPER AND BASIL

P. 234 • SERVES 4

Preparation: 25 min • **Marinating time:** 1 hr

Cooking time: 15 min

60g (2oz) piece ginger, 3 garlic cloves, 2 duck breasts, 8 tbsp soy sauce, 2 tbsp tamarind sauce, 2 red (bell) peppers, 15 basil leaves, 2 tbsp sunflower oil, 1 small red chilli, 4 lemon tree leaves, 2 bunches of fresh pepper, cooking oil, salt and pepper

Peel and grate the ginger, then peel and chop the garlic. Remove the fat from the duck breasts then chop into thin slices and marinate for 1 hour with the garlic, ginger, 4 tbsp soy sauce and the tamarind sauce. Trim, deseed and chop the (bell) peppers into large strips. Prepare and heat a deep-fryer to 100°C/ 212°F. Add the basil to the hot oil and fry for 1 minute then drain on kitchen paper (paper towels). Keep warm. Heat the sunflower oil to smoking point in a large wok. Fry the duck strips and their marinade in the hot oil then add the strips of pepper, the whole chilli, the lemon tree leaves and the bunches of pepper and stir-fry everything together until browned. When the ingredients begin to stick to the wok, add the remaining soy sauce. Serve the duck piping hot covered with its cooking juices, garnished with the basil leaves and served with rice.

ROAST DUCK SOUP WITH EGG NOODLES

P. 235 • SERVES 4

Preparation: 20 min • **Cooking time:** 5 min

5 spring onion (scallion) stems, 400g (14oz) fresh egg noodles (wheat), 400g (14oz) roast duck or the remains of a Cheat's Peking duck (see recipe opposite), 1 litre (1¾ pints/4 cups) homemade chicken broth (see p.79) or use a stock cube

Trim and chop the spring onions (scallions). Drop the noodles into a large pan of boiling salted water for 3–5 minutes, then taste to check if they are cooked. Drain and divide among bowls, add the duck then pour in the hot broth. Sprinkle with the spring onions (scallions) and leave to stand for a few minutes before serving.

CHEAT'S PEKING DUCK WITH HOISIN SAUCE

P. 236 • SERVES 4–6

Preparation: 1 hr • Marinating **time:** overnight

Cooking time: 30–45 min • **Resting time:** 2 hr

I bunch of coriander (cilantro), 50g (1¾oz) piece ginger, 20g (¾oz) piece galangal, 3 garlic cloves, 2 lemongrass stalks, 2 tbsp five-spice mixture, 1 tbsp ground coriander, 1 Barbary duck, 6 tbsp soy sauce, 8 tbsp hoisin sauce

Rinse and remove part of the stalks of the coriander (cilantro). Peel the ginger and galangal, then peel the garlic and lemongrass. Mix these ingredients to a smooth paste with the five-spice and the ground coriander. Pierce the duck with a fork (except underneath) and baste it inside and out with the paste. Wrap it in clingfilm (plastic wrap) and leave to marinate overnight in a cool place. Clean the duck, sprinkle over a little soy sauce, wrap it in clingfilm (plastic wrap) again and steam for 30 minutes, then remove the clingfilm. Wrap the duck in kitchen paper (paper towels) or in a clean cloth and leave to rest and dry out for 2 hours. Preheat the oven to 200°C/400°F/Gas Mark 6. Using a brush, baste the duck with hoisin sauce then place it on a grill (broiler) rack set over a roasting tin. Roast in the oven for about 45 minutes, basting at least once with the sauce. The skin should turn golden and crispy. Remove from the oven and leave to cool. Cut into small pieces and serve with white rice, stir-fried Chinese cabbage and hoisin sauce.

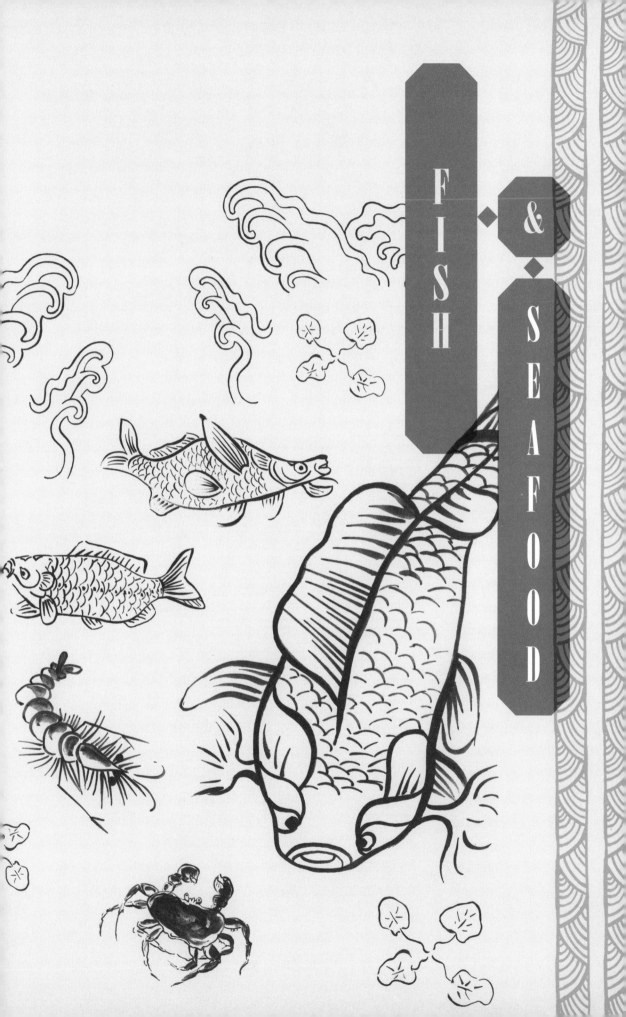

FISH & SEAFOOD

FISH & SEAFOOD

From Northeast to Southeast China, as well as in Southeast Asia, fish and seafood are eaten in very large quantities. The residents of Hong Kong are among the largest consumers of shellfish in the world, most of which is farmed. The Chinese also eat a lot of farmed fish, especially freshwater species such as carp. Fish is also a key ingredient of many different sauces (nuoc-mâm, oyster sauce, etc.), and dried fish features regularly in Asian food, as it's a useful way to preserve the fish. The consistency of dried fish may be somewhat cardboard-like, but is not unpleasant. To fully savour Asian cuisine, you have to learn to appreciate foreign textures – Thai cuisine combines these powerful flavours with the freshness of herbs and the sharpness of green mango prepared in a salad, while in Singapore, *chilli crab* – fried crab claws coated with a spicy sweet-and-sour tomato sauce and served with a type of steamed bun

Previous page: Every Chinese restaurant has its own aquarium: customers choose their own fish which is then cooked to order (New York).

called *mantou* – is an emblematic recipe of the city. You suck and lick every last morsel off the claws! Another surprising dish, which is widespread in the city-state, is fish-head curry. Originally from the Indian peninsula, this dish has been enriched along the way.

Restaurants with fish tanks are a Chinese custom that is rarely found in the West. Diners choose their own fish, which is immediately whisked away into the kitchens before quickly coming back on an oval plate, garnished with various herbs and other sauces. The freshness is guaranteed, and the taste? Obviously, if the fish has spent several weeks in a tank, it will not have the subtlety of a freshly caught sea bass, for example, but Asians do not share the Western conception of fish, and besides, raw fish and seafood are extremely rare. Not everyone can eat like the Japanese!

View of Manhattan's towers from
New York's Chinatown

Clams cooking in New York's
Chinatown

Entrance to Montreal's
Chinatown

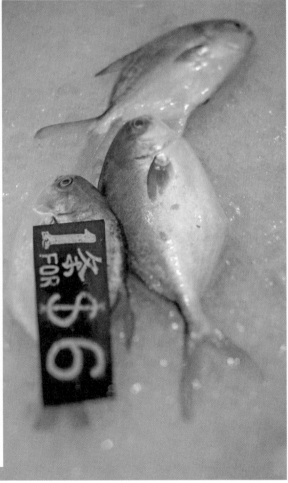

Small dried fish served in a salad

Fresh fish sold at a market in
New York

FRIED SHRIMP WITH HOT SAUCE

SERVES 4–6

Preparation: 20 min • **Marinating time:** 1 hr • **Cooking time:** 10 min

---

20 raw prawns (shrimp)

5 tbsp soy sauce

1 tbsp cornflour (cornstarch)

4 tbsp groundnut (peanut) oil

1 red (bell) pepper

1 green (bell) pepper

1 garlic clove

1 sweet onion

2 tbsp chilli sauce

Peel the prawns (shrimp) keeping the tails on, remove the black vein from along the back of each prawn (shrimp), then rinse and dry the prawns (shrimp).

Mix the prawns (shrimp), soy sauce, cornflour (cornstarch) and 1 tbsp groundnut (peanut) oil together in a bowl, cover and leave the prawns (shrimp) to marinate for 1 hour.

Trim, deseed and chop the (bell) peppers, then peel and chop the garlic and onion.

Heat the remaining oil in a large wok and fry the prawns (shrimp) and their marinade in the hot oil. Add the (bell) peppers, garlic and onion and stir-fry for 5 minutes. Pour in the chilli sauce, stir and add a little water. Continue to stir-fry for 2 minutes, still over a high heat.

Turn off the heat and arrange the prawns (shrimp) with the sauce on a large serving plate. Serve with white rice.

CHINESE
STEAMED FISH

P. 254 • SERVES 5–6

Preparation: 40 min • **Cooking time:** 25 min

4 garlic cloves, 50g (1¾oz) piece ginger, 1 leek (just the white part), 1 bunch of coriander (cilantro), 1 bunch of chives, 4 tbsp sunflower oil, 1 tsp caster (superfine) sugar, 50ml (2fl oz/ scant ¼ cup) soy sauce, 1 large trout (about 2kg/4½lb), salt and pepper

Peel and chop the garlic. Peel the ginger and chop this and the leek into thin 'julienne' strips (small sticks). Rinse and chop the coriander (cilantro) with its stalks. Rinse the chives and cut into sections. Heat the oil in a large pan and fry the garlic until brown, then drain onto a plate. Reduce the heat and add the julienne vegetable strips. Cook for 1 minute then turn off the heat and pour in the sugar, soy sauce and a large glass of water. Leave to rest. Wash, clean and season the trout then steam for 25 minutes. Alternatively, cook in a fish kettle with boiling water. When it is well cooked, put into a large serving dish. Cover with the sauce, sprinkle over the garlic, coriander (cilantro) and chives. Serve with white rice.

STEAMED SHANGHAI
HAIRY CRABS

P. 255 • SERVES 4

Preparation: 10 min • **Cooking time:** 25 min

50g (1¾oz) piece ginger, 8 tbsp rice vinegar, 2 tbsp caster (superfine) sugar, 4 large freshwater crabs

Peel and finely grate the ginger, then mix with the vinegar and caster (superfine) sugar. Set aside. If the crabs are still live, tie up their claws with string and steam them for about 25 minutes. Serve the crabmeat seasoned with the sweet ginger vinegar.

STEAMED CRAB WITH VIETNAMESE SAUCE AND KUMQUATS

P. 256 • SERVES 4

Preparation: 25 min • **Resting time:** 1 hr

Cooking time: 20 min

12 small frozen crabs
For the sauce: 1 garlic clove, 5 kumquats, 1 small chilli, 3 tbsp nuoc-mâm, 3 tbsp rice vinegar, 1 tbsp caster (superfine) sugar, 6 tbsp warm water

Peel and chop the garlic. Cut the kumquats into thin slices. Deseed and slice the chilli. Mix the nuoc-mâm, rice vinegar, sugar and warm water together in a bowl. Add the kumquats, chilli and garlic. Mix and leave to rest for 1 hour in a cold place. Steam the crabs for 20 minutes then shell them and serve the meat with the sauce.

CHILLI CRAB

P. 257 • SERVES 4

Preparation: 20 min • **Cooking time:** 20 min

1 bunch of coriander (cilantro), 4 large crabs (mud crabs or edible crabs), 2 heads of garlic, 50ml (2fl oz/scant ¼ cup) groundnut (peanut) oil, 150g (5½oz) red chilli sauce, 150g (5½oz) ketchup

Rinse and chop the coriander (cilantro). Put the crabs into a pan of boiling water for 1 minute. Drain and leave to cool. Remove the claws. Open the crabs by lifting off the shell. Peel the garlic. Heat the oil in a wok and fry the garlic for 1 minute. Add the crabmeat and claws. Pour over 300ml (10fl oz/1¼ cups) water, cover and cook for 10 minutes. Add the chilli sauce, stir and cook for another few minutes. Add the ketchup and cook for another 5 minutes. Arrange the crabs in a large dish. Mix the sauce well then pour it over the crabs. Garnish with coriander (cilantro) and serve with white rice.

FRIED SQUID WITH SPRING ONION

SERVES 4

Preparation: 20 min • **Cooking time:** 10 min

8–10 fresh squid with tentacles (cleaned and ready to cook)
2 garlic cloves
10g (¼oz) piece ginger

6 spring onion (scallion) stems
3 tbsp Chinese wine (from Shaoxing)

6 tbsp light soy sauce
2 tbsp sunflower oil

Chop the squid into small pieces. Peel and chop the garlic. Peel and chop the ginger. Rinse the spring onions (scallions), dry and chop them roughly.

Pour the wine and soy sauce into a wok, bring to the boil then carefully drop in the squid for 1 minute. Drain and reduce the cooking liquid by half. Set the cooking juices aside in a bowl. Wash and dry the wok.

Heat the sunflower oil in the wok and fry the squid for 1 minute. Add the spring onion (scallion), garlic and ginger and cook for 3–4 minutes, stirring all the time. Pour over the reserved cooking juices, stir and turn off the heat.

Arrange the squid with the sauce in a shallow serving dish and serve with white rice.

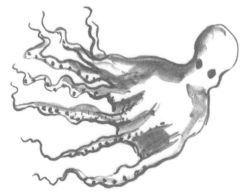

DEEP-FRIED FISH WITH GARLIC AND CHILLI SAUCE

SERVES 4

Preparation: 25 min • **Cooking time:** 30 min

2 garlic cloves

8 tbsp soy sauce

1 tbsp sesame oil

400g (14oz/2½ cups) rice flour

2 tbsp turmeric

2 eggs

4 small plaice (flounder)

(cleaned and skinned)

2 tbsp chilli paste

cooking oil

Peel and chop the garlic. Mix the soy sauce, sesame oil and chopped garlic together in a bowl.

Mix the rice flour with the turmeric in a large bowl, then gradually beat in a little water until you have a smooth, but not too liquid batter. Add the eggs and mix.

Prepare and heat a deep-fryer. Dip a fish into the batter, then carefully lower it into the hot oil and fry for 6–8 minutes, turning from time to time. Remove the fish from the oil with a slotted spoon and keep it warm. Repeat with the remaining fish.

Drain the fish and serve piping hot with the chilli paste and the garlicky soy sauce.

RECIPE
PAGE
268

STUFFED CRAB WITH PORK AND RICE NOODLES

P. 264 • SERVES 4

Preparation: 40 min • **Cooking time:** 20 min

4 spring onion (scallion) stems, 1 garlic clove, 100g (3½oz) sausage meat, 200g (7oz) crabmeat (fresh or canned), 1 egg, 2 tbsp nuoc-mâm, 100g (3½oz) rice vermicelli, 4 crab shells (or ramekins) *For the sauce:* 1 small red chilli, deseeded and chopped, leaves from a few coriander (cilantro) sprigs, 2 tbsp warm water, 2 tbsp nuoc-mâm, 30g (1oz) caster (superfine) sugar, 2 tbsp rice vinegar, juice of 1 lime

Preheat the oven to 170°C/340°F/Gas Mark 3. Rinse and chop the spring onions (scallions), then peel and chop the garlic. In a bowl, mix together the sausage meat, garlic, spring onion (scallion), crab, egg, nuoc-mâm and vermicelli, chopped into pieces. Stuff the crab shells with this mixture. Put them in the oven for 20 minutes then pop under the grill (broiler) for a few minutes to brown the tops. Meanwhile, make the sauce by mixing all the ingredients together. Serve the stuffed crab with the sauce and white rice.

FRIED FISH WITH SWEET-AND-SOUR SAUCE

P. 265 • SERVES 4

Preparation: 35 min • **Marinating time:** overnight
Cooking time: 25 min

4 whole fish (sea bass, trout, red or grey mullet, sea bream), cleaned and scaled, 2 tbsp coarse salt, 10 spring onion (scallion) stems, 5 baby leeks, 5 tbsp ketchup, 6 tbsp soy sauce, 1 tbsp cornflour (cornstarch), 1 tsp sesame oil, 500ml (18fl oz/2 cups) fish stock (see p.72), 300g (10½oz/scant 2½ cups) flour, 1 tbsp chilli sauce, cooking oil

Make deep cuts into the flesh on both sides of the fish. Cover with coarse salt and leave to marinate overnight. Rinse then chop the spring onions (scallions) and leeks. Mix the ketchup, soy sauce, cornflour (cornstarch) and sesame oil in a pan. Add the stock and bring to the boil, then cook over a low heat for 5 minutes, stirring. Wash the fish under cold water to get rid of the salt then dry and dip in flour. Prepare and heat a deep-fryer. Lower the fish into the hot oil and fry each one for 4–5 minutes until golden. Arrange the fish in a dish and pour over the boiling sweet-and-sour sauce. Sprinkle with spring onions (scallions) and leek. Serve with rice.

'CHAO TOM'

P. 267 • SERVES 4

Preparation: 45 min • **Marinating time:** 30 min

Cooking time: 15 min

50g (1¾oz) pork belly (bacon), cut into small cubes, 600g (1lb 7oz) large peeled prawns (shrimp), 80ml (3fl oz/⅓ cup) coconut milk, 2 garlic cloves, 5 spring onions (scallions), 40g (1½oz/¼ cup) roasted peanuts, salt and pepper, 4 sugar cane sticks (15 x 1.5cm/6–⅝in)
For the liver sauce: 20g (¾oz/1½ tbsp) sticky rice, 3 garlic cloves, ¼ of a bunch of spring onions (scallions), ¼ of a bunch of coriander (cilantro), 50g (1¾oz) pig's liver, 1 tbsp groundnut (peanut) oil, 1 tbsp nuoc-mâm, 1 small red chilli, 1 tsp roasted peanuts

Cook the bacon in a very low oven for 1 hour until transparent but neither golden nor dried out. Chop roughly and keep warm. Meanwhile, peel the prawns (shrimp) and marinate for 30 minutes in the coconut milk. Peel and chop the garlic. Wash then chop the spring onion (scallion). In a food mixer, mix the prawns (shrimp), bacon, spring onion (scallion) and garlic to a smooth paste. Cover the sugar cane sticks with a thick coating of the paste and cook for 15 minutes on the barbecue or 20 minutes in the oven at 180°C/350°F/Gas Mark 4. Meanwhile, make the liver sauce. Cook the rice in 10cm (4 inches) water. Peel and chop the garlic and chop the spring onions (scallions) and coriander (cilantro). Chop the pig's liver into small pieces and fry in the oil with the garlic, spring onion (scallion) and coriander (cilantro) for 5 minutes. Add the rice and a glass of water. Boil for 5 minutes then add the nuoc-mâm. Mix with a hand blender. Sprinkle over the chopped chilli and peanuts. Serve with the sugar cane sticks sprinkled with roasted peanuts.

DEEP-FRIED PRAWNS

P. 266 • SERVES 4

Preparation: 30 min • **Cooking time:** 20 min

125g (4½oz/1 cup) flour, ½ packet of yeast, pinch of salt, 1 tbsp groundnut (peanut) oil, 1 egg, 50ml (2fl oz/scant ¼ cup) water, 12–16 large raw prawns (shrimp), cooking oil
For the sauce: 1 garlic clove, 1 small red chilli, a few coriander (cilantro) sprigs, 2 tbsp water, 2 tbsp nuoc-mâm, 30g (1oz/2 tbsp) caster (superfine) sugar, 2 tbsp rice vinegar, juice of 1 lime

For the sauce, peel and chop the garlic, chop the chilli and remove the coriander (cilantro) leaves from the stalks. Mix the sauce ingredients together. For the batter, combine the flour, yeast, salt and oil in a bowl. Loosen the mixture with the water then add the beaten egg. Leave to rest. Peel the prawns (shrimp), keeping the tails on. Prepare and heat a deep-fryer. Dip the prawns (shrimp) one at a time into the batter, then into the hot oil. Let them expand and fry until golden. Drain and serve with the sauce on the side.

FRIED FISH WITH BROTH AND CORIANDER

SERVES 4

Preparation: 25 min • **Marinating time:** overnight • **Cooking time:** 5 min

4 whole fish (sea bass, trout, red or grey mullet, sea bream) cleaned and scaled
2 tbsp coarse salt
2 bunches of coriander (cilantro)

30g (1oz) piece ginger
10 tbsp soy sauce
1 tsp sesame oil
500ml (18fl oz/2 cups) fish stock (frozen or powdered)

300g (10½oz/scant 2½ cups) flour
cooking oil

Make deep cuts in both sides of the fish. Cover with coarse salt then leave to marinate overnight. Rinse and chop the coriander (cilantro). Peel and grate the ginger.

Put the ginger, soy sauce, sesame oil and stock in a saucepan, bring to the boil, then turn off the heat and set aside.

Wash the fish under cold running water to remove the salt then dry on a clean cloth. Put the flour in a shallow dish, then add the fish and turn to coat on both sides.

Prepare and heat a deep-fryer then carefully lower the fish one at a time into the hot oil and deep-fry for about 3–4 minutes until golden. Drain on kitchen paper (paper towels).

Arrange the fish in a large shallow dish and cover with the soy sauce broth. Sprinkle with the chopped coriander (cilantro) and serve piping hot with white rice.

SALT AND PEPPER PRAWNS

SERVES 4

Preparation: 10 min • **Cooking time:** 5 min

1 tsp fine salt

1 tsp ground Sichuan pepper

1 tsp caster (superfine) sugar

200g (7oz/generous 1½ cups) flour

20 raw frozen prawns (shrimp) with their heads and tails on

chilli sauce

cooking oil

Mix the salt, Sichuan pepper and sugar in a bowl and set aside.

Prepare and heat a deep-fryer. Put the flour in a shallow dish, dip the unpeeled prawns (shrimp) in the flour then carefully lower them into the hot oil and deep-fry for 5 minutes.

Drain the prawns (shrimp) on kitchen paper (paper towels). Arrange in a serving dish then season with the salt, pepper and sugar mixture. Serve immediately with chilli sauce.

FRIED PRAWNS WITH PINEAPPLE

SERVES 4–6

Preparation: 35 min • Marinating time: 1 hr • Cooking time: 20 min

20 raw frozen prawns (shrimp)

2 tbsp soy sauce

1 bunch of coriander (cilantro)

1 sweet onion

10 spring onion (scallion) stems

1 red (bell) pepper

1 green (bell) pepper

1 x 250g (9oz) can pineapple
in syrup

250ml (9fl oz/generous 1 cup)
tomato sauce

2 tbsp rice vinegar

1 tbsp caster (superfine) sugar

3 tbsp oyster sauce

1 tbsp cornflour (cornstarch)

200g (7oz/generous 1½ cups)
flour

1 tbsp groundnut (peanut) oil

cooking oil

Peel the prawns (shrimp) and marinate for 1 hour in a bowl with the soy sauce.

Rinse and roughly chop the coriander (cilantro), peel and chop the onion, then rinse and roughly chop the spring onions (scallions). Trim, deseed and chop the (bell) peppers, then drain the pineapple slices and cut into pieces, reserving the syrup.

Put the tomato sauce, vinegar, sugar, pineapple syrup and oyster sauce together in a pan. Whisk in the cornflour (cornstarch) and bring to the boil. Cook for 5 minutes, stirring all the time, then turn off the heat.

Prepare and heat a deep-fryer. Drain the prawns (shrimp), dip them in the flour then carefully lower them into the hot oil and deep-fry for 4–5 minutes. Drain on a plate lined with kitchen paper (paper towels).

Heat the groundnut (peanut) oil in a large wok and fry the onion, pineapple pieces and (bell) peppers for 3 minutes, or until brown. Add the sweet-and-sour sauce and the fried prawns (shrimp), stir everything together over a high heat for 1 minute, then arrange on a large plate. Sprinkle with spring onion (scallion) and coriander (cilantro) and serve with white rice.

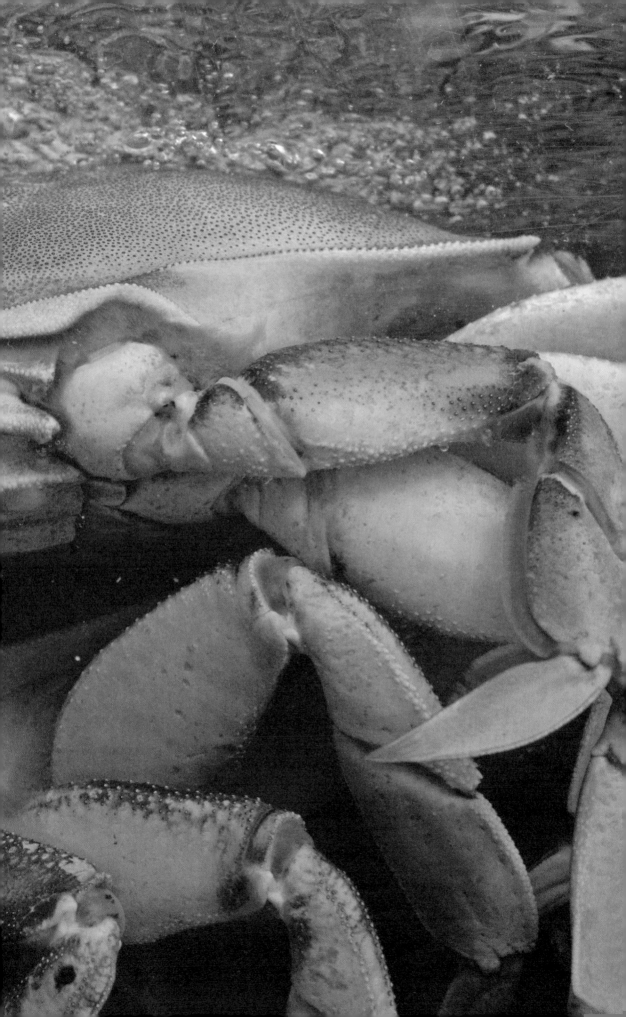

WEIRD

The 'strange' ingredients of Chinese food have become something of a cliché: insects, jelly-fish, dogs, cats and snakes are all served in China, Vietnam and elsewhere in the East. But doesn't every nation have its own peculiarities when it comes to food? To the English, it seems strange to eat frogs; the Americans could not imagine eating rabbit, so why not try exposing our taste buds to the flavours appreciated by others with a view to both satisfying our curiosity and enriching our palate?

WONDERFUL

IS IT EDIBLE?

A proverb states that the Chinese eat anything that flies, except for planes, and anything that has four legs, except for public benches. It is true that in China the scope of culinary possibilities is extremely large, including, for example, ducks' tongues and webbed feet, jellyfish, insects, fried tarantula, scorpion kebabs, star fish, snakes and snake eggs, dogs, cats, coypus (river rats), shark fins, incubating eggs, sea cucumbers and century-old eggs. (The latter are eggs preserved in a mixture rich in lime, rice husk, ash and salt. This changes their colour to a greenish brown, giving them the look of rotten eggs, hence their name.)

Some foods that are considered to be luxury dishes in Asia, such as shark fins or swallows' nests, are rare and frowned upon in the West. You will definitely not find

Previous page: Chinese New Year in New York's Chinatown.

either on the menu in Western restaurants. Found originally in the East of Malaysia, swallows nests are made of
a gelatinous substance secreted by some swifts to build
their nest. Once cooked, these nests disintegrate into several small parts used to make various soups and dishes.
The Chinese credit them with many properties, claiming
that they improve both digestion and life expectancy.

In the West, you are more likely to find a salad of
jellyfish tentacles. The flavour is not particularly strong,
but the texture is extremely crisp with a consistency similar to poultry cartilage. You might also come across moult-
ing crabs, served fried, or sea cucumbers that have been
either fried or cooked in a casserole.

Bags of small dried fish

Shark fins, the sale of which is banned in Europe but still
authorized in New York.

Dried
giant squid

Durian, the 'king of
fruits', is especially
popular for Chinese
New Year festivities

Dried abalones on sale in a
Chinatown grocery store

Dried swallows nests, very highly valued for the preparation of soups

Opposite: Presentation of scorpions, seahorses and starfish for tasting (Hong Kong)

Fresh jellyfish

Live frogs

Sign for a shop selling shark meat and fins and other unusual items

Coloured agar agar

Canned pork rind

Spicy crab paste used to flavour soups

Dried squid meat

Dried sea cucumber

Marinated vegetables

DARNES DE
REQUIN PEAU BLEUE
BLUE SHARK SLICES
Poids: 1kg (900g net déglacé)

PREMIUM
OCEAN GIRL
ABALONE
NET WEIGHT 15oz (425g)

Canned abalone

Frozen shark steaks

SLOW-COOKED SEA CUCUMBER WITH PUMPKIN

SERVES 4

Preparation: 15 min • **Cooking time:** 25 min

---

4 large florets of broccoli
1 garlic clove
100g (3½oz) pumpkin flesh
4 large sea cucumbers, ready to cook, canned or dried

1 tbsp groundnut (peanut) oil
200ml (9fl oz/generous 1 cup) chicken stock
1 tbsp oyster sauce
1 tbsp rice vinegar

1 tsp cornflour (cornstarch)
1 tsp dried shrimp
egg powder
salt and pepper

Rinse the broccoli then steam very gently for about 20 minutes, or until cooked. Peel and chop the garlic and cut the pumpkin into small cubes.

Bring a pan of water to the boil then drop in the sea cucumbers and cook for 5 minutes. Drain and plunge them into cold water to remove the salt.

Meanwhile, heat the groundnut (peanut) oil in a large wok. Fry the pumpkin and garlic in the hot oil. Brown slightly for 1 minute then pour over the chicken stock, oyster sauce and rice vinegar and simmer for 25 minutes over a low heat.

Dissolve the cornflour (cornstarch) in a little water before adding it to the wok, then stir and mix everything thoroughly with a hand-held blender. Drain the sea cucumbers then add them to the sauce. Bring to the boil then rduce the heat and simmer for 1 minute. Check the seasoning.

Arrange the sea cucumbers on large plates. Add the broccoli florets and pour over the sauce. Sprinkle over the dried shrimp egg powder and serve with a bowl of rice.

CHICKEN FEET

SERVES 4

Preparation: 30 min • **Cooking time:** 1 hr 15 min

500g (1lb 2oz) fresh chicken feet
2 tsp caster (superfine) sugar
3 tbsp soy sauce

3 tbsp oyster sauce
1 small dried chilli (or a large
pinch of chilli powder)

1 cinnamon stick
2 cloves
cooking oil

Scrub the chicken feet under cold running water with a small brush to get them nice and clean, then dry them one by one on a clean cloth (you can pull out the claws at this point if you wish).

Prepare and heat a deep-fryer. Carefully lower the chicken feet into the hot oil and deep-fry until golden, then drain thoroughly on kitchen paper (paper towels).

Place the chicken feet in a wok, add the sugar, soy sauce and oyster sauce and cook over a high heat to caramelize everything. Add the chilli and spices then cover with water and simmer for 1 hour over a low heat. Drain the feet and serve warm.

RECIPE
PAGE
302

RECIPE PAGE 302

CURRIED FISH HEAD

P. 298 • SERVES 6

Preparation: 15 min • **Cooking time:** 40 min

100g (3½oz) okra (ladies fingers), 1 large meaty fish head (+ a couple of large steaks if you prefer more flesh), 3 onions, 4 garlic cloves, 20g (¾oz) piece ginger, 2 tbsp sunflower oil, 4 tbsp special fish curry powder*, 4 ripe tomatoes, 4 curry leaves, 1 small chilli, 500ml (18fl oz/2 cups) coconut milk, 1 tbsp tamarind paste

Trim the okra (ladies fingers), rinse and chop into pieces. Wash and dry the fish head. Peel and chop the onions and garlic.

Peel the ginger and cut into thin slices. Heat the oil in a large pan and fry the garlic, onions and ginger in the hot oil. When browned, add the curry powder, chopped tomatoes, curry leaves and sliced chilli. Stir and cook for a few minutes then reduce the heat and add the fish head and okra (ladies fingers). Pour in 2 large glasses of water, bring back to the boil then reduce the heat and simmer for 25 minutes over a low heat. Serve hot with a bowl of white rice.

*To make the special homemade fish curry powder, mix 50g (1¾oz) ground coriander with 1½ tbsp ground cumin, 2 tsp chilli powder and 2 tbsp ground rosemary.

STEAMED TENTACLES WITH SOY SAUCE

P. 299 • SERVES 4

Preparation: 10 min • **Marinating time:** 2 hr

Cooking time: 20 min

2 garlic cloves, 30g (1oz) piece ginger, 400g (14oz) medium cuttlefish, octopus or squid tentacles (you can also use squid rings), 8 tbsp soy sauce, 2 tbsp sesame oil

Peel the garlic and ginger then chop the garlic and grate the ginger. Mix the tentacles with the soy sauce, sesame oil, ginger and garlic. Marinate for 2 hours in a cold place. Drain the tentacles and steam for 20 minutes. Strain the marinade and set aside. Serve the tentacles hot and slightly firm and season them with the marinade.

FROGS' LEGS WITH COCONUT MILK AND BASIL

P. 300 • SERVES 6

Preparation: 20 min • **Marinating time:** 1 hr

Cooking time: 25 min

1 red (bell) pepper, 1 bunch of Thai basil, 2 garlic cloves, 2 lemongrass stalks, 800g (1lb 12oz) frogs' legs (fresh or frozen), 1 tbsp nuoc-mâm, ½ tsp caster (superfine) sugar, 2 tbsp light soy sauce, 50ml (2fl oz/scant ¼ cup) coconut milk, 1 tbsp groundnut (peanut) oil

Trim the (bell) pepper, deseed and slice. Rinse the basil and remove the stalks. Peel and chop the garlic and lemongrass. Mix the frogs' legs with the garlic, nuoc-mâm, sugar, soy sauce and lemongrass and marinate for 1 hour in a cold place. Heat the oil in a large wok. Fry the slices of (bell) pepper for a few minutes in the hot oil then add the frogs' legs and their marinade and cook over a high heat, stirring all the time. When the marinade has reduced by three quarters, add the coconut milk. Reduce for another 5 minutes, stirring, then add the basil leaves. Turn off the heat, mix and leave for 1 minute. Serve with rice.

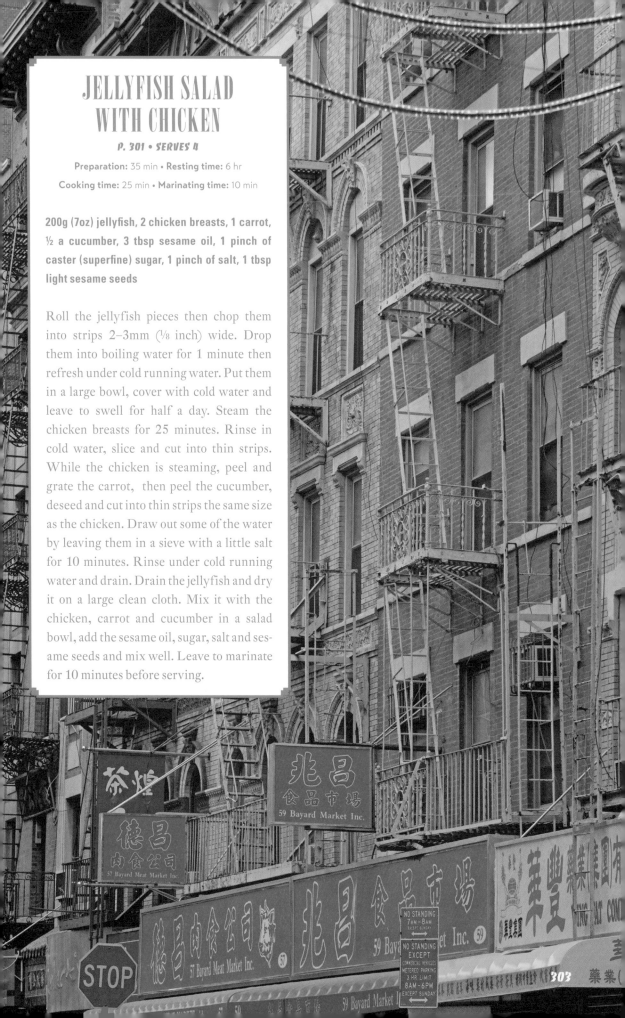

JELLYFISH SALAD WITH CHICKEN

P. 301 • SERVES 4

Preparation: 35 min • **Resting time:** 6 hr

Cooking time: 25 min • **Marinating time:** 10 min

200g (7oz) jellyfish, 2 chicken breasts, 1 carrot, ½ a cucumber, 3 tbsp sesame oil, 1 pinch of caster (superfine) sugar, 1 pinch of salt, 1 tbsp light sesame seeds

Roll the jellyfish pieces then chop them into strips 2–3mm (⅛ inch) wide. Drop them into boiling water for 1 minute then refresh under cold running water. Put them in a large bowl, cover with cold water and leave to swell for half a day. Steam the chicken breasts for 25 minutes. Rinse in cold water, slice and cut into thin strips. While the chicken is steaming, peel and grate the carrot, then peel the cucumber, deseed and cut into thin strips the same size as the chicken. Draw out some of the water by leaving them in a sieve with a little salt for 10 minutes. Rinse under cold running water and drain. Drain the jellyfish and dry it on a large clean cloth. Mix it with the chicken, carrot and cucumber in a salad bowl, add the sesame oil, sugar, salt and sesame seeds and mix well. Leave to marinate for 10 minutes before serving.

Seasongings Corner
自助調味處

THE SEASONINGS

Asian seasonings are a complex business, as there are so many of them and they are radically different to our own. You also need to bear in mind that Asian countries do not all share the same tastes when it comes to chillies. The Thai people are such fans of chilli that it can be hard to eat in the streets of Bangkok because the food is so hot. In Cambodia, Vietnam and Laos, on the other hand, the food is less spicy. As for China, it all depends on the region and the individual dish: the cuisine of the Southwest (Hunan and Sichuan provinces) is very hot.

Soy sauce and nuoc-mâm (fish sauce) are two mainstream seasonings in Asian cuisine. There is a traditional and an industrial version of soy sauce, and in the West, you find it in varying degrees of light/strong. Sweet-and-sour chilli sauce, concentrated tamarind sauce with its sour flavour, sesame oil, chilli oil, rice wine and vinegar are all frequently used. Thick plum sauce is used to flavour dumplings. The renowned thick, brown oyster sauce was discovered by chance by a Cantonese man, Lee Kum Kee. Originally it was made using oysters, but today's more industrial versions are vegetable based. And finally, sriracha sauce, found on many Asian tables but originating from Thailand, is made of chillies, garlic, vinegar, salt and sugar and will add spice to any dish.

TRADITIONAL SHARK'S FIN SOUP

SERVES 4

Preparation: 1 hr • **Marinating time:** 1 hr 30 min • **Cooking time:** 1 hr 15 min

---

50g (1¾oz) dried shark's fin (shark fins are prohibited in the West, so either replace it with imitation shark's fin, cellophane noodles, fresh crabmeat or 20g/¾oz fresh or frozen skate wing)

100g (3½oz) pork loin
3 dried black mushrooms
80g (3oz) bamboo shoots
20g (¾oz) piece ginger
2 tbsp cornflour (cornstarch)
2 tbsp soy sauce

3 tbsp sherry
1.5 litres (2½ pints/6⅓ cups) chicken stock
a few leaves of cooked pak choi
8 cooked scallops with roes

Soak the shark fins for 1 hour in a bowl of cold water.

Chop the pork and set aside. Soak the mushrooms in a bowl of warm water for 15 minutes to rehydrate them then drain and chop them. Drain the bamboo shoots and chop them in the same way. Peel the ginger then cut into thin slices.

Bring a pan of water to the boil. Add the ginger and shark fins and simmer for 1 hour (just 10 minutes if using skate wings), then drain the fins onto a plate.

Whisk 1 tbsp cornflour (cornstarch) with the soy sauce and sherry in a bowl, add the pork and let it marinate for 30 minutes.

Whisk the remaining cornflour (cornstarch) with a little chicken stock. Bring the rest of the stock to the boil in a pan. Add the marinated meat and stir, then add the shark fins and simmer for 10 minutes. Finally, add the cornflour (cornstarch) mixture, stir it in carefully then turn off the heat.

Arrange the mushrooms, bamboo shoots, ginger and pork in the bowls. Place the shark fins on top then add the broth. Garnish with the pak choi leaves and cooked scallops with roes.

TOFU WITH 100-YEAR-OLD EGGS

SERVES 6

Preparation: 15 min

10 spring onion (scallion) stems

300g (10½oz) fresh tofu

2 x 100-year-old eggs

5 tbsp soy sauce

Wash and chop the spring onions (scallions). Drain the tofu and cut into thick slices, then leave it to drain in a colander.

Peel the 100-year-old eggs then chop them roughly with a large knife.

Arrange the tofu slices in a large serving dish, place the chopped eggs on top and cover with soy sauce.

Sprinkle over the spring onions (scallions) and serve as a starter with chopsticks.

RECIPE
PAGE
312

SLOW-COOKED ABALONES WITH ASPARAGUS

P. 311 • SERVES 6

Preparation: 25 min • **Cooking time:** 45 min

12 large asparagus spears, 6 large canned abalones, 250ml (9fl oz/generous 1 cup) chicken stock, 4 tbsp light soy sauce, 6 tbsp oyster sauce or abalone sauce, salt and pepper

Bring a pan of salted water to the boil. Trim the asparagus spears then plunge them into the boiling water and cook for 3 minutes. Drain and refresh under cold running water. Set aside.

Drain the abalones and pour the juice into a large wok. Add the chicken stock and soy sauce, bring to the boil then add the abalones and simmer for 45 minutes, basting regularly with the cooking liquid. Drain the abalones onto a plate. Reduce the sauce by half before adding the oyster sauce. Check the seasoning.

Drop the asparagus and the abalones into the sauce to reheat them, then arrange on large plates, pour over the sauce and serve with white rice.

SOY SAUCE

There are several different qualities of soy sauce. The most authentic sauce is made with soybean seeds, which are boiled first to soften them. Next, they are placed in barrels and wheat flour is added, then they are left to ferment for a week in a room where the temperature is strictly controlled. The barrels are then moved outside and exposed to the sun for three months. After that, salt water is added to the barrels and they are left out in the sun for a further three months. It is at this stage that the juice is collected from the barrels. This is what is known as premium soy sauce.

At this point, more salt water can be added, and the mixture left for another three months. The liquid collected after this is still soy sauce but will be less concentrated than the first batch.

The quality of the soy sauce depends on the fermentation period, for which the temperature is kept secret. Just as there are cellar masters for wine or spirits, so too there are masters for soy sauce, who watch over the fermentation process night and day. Real soy sauce is 100% natural, made of water, salt and soybean seeds. Take note: Chinese soy sauce has no sugar, unlike the Japanese variety.

HACCP QUALIFY

VEGETABLES, RICE

&

SIDE DISHES

VEGETABLES & RICE

Vegetables are served separately and ordered as additional dishes to meat or fish. Black mushrooms, oyster mushrooms and other mushrooms are frequently served as side dishes. So, too, is water spinach, which in the West is often found in recipes flavoured with garlic, and pak choi and Chinese cabbage, which is often cooked in oyster sauce. Tofu – which may be fresh, dried or smoked – can be steamed, fried, or stewed and served hot or cold. It is often compared to cheese, as it is made from curdled soya milk. Also on the menu are bamboo shoots and lotus root.

The mainstay of Asian cuisine is rice, which is the third most produced cereal in the world, after corn and wheat. China is the world's largest rice producer, followed by India, although Vietnam and Thailand are also big rice exporters. There are many different varieties of rice: while it is round in Japan, rice is long and fragrant in Thailand. There is also a type of sticky rice with quite different starch components to those found in other rice varieties.

Rice-based recipes are extremely numerous, including plain rice, fried rice, the famous Cantonese-style fried rice, *congee* (a rice soup eaten at breakfast in China and South-east Asia) and the Lao crispy rice salad. Rice goes just as well in a salad as it does with noodles, meat, vegetables or fish. In many countries, meals end with a bowl of rice that should not be finished; this lets the host know that you have been well fed and are no longer hungry.

Pak choi cooked in a wok

Kimchi
(cabbage fermented in chilli)

Steamed stuffed pumpkin

Green papaya and
dried beef rolls

Lotus root slices preserved in
soy sauce and sprinkled with
sesame seeds

Fresh garlic stems fried
with peanuts

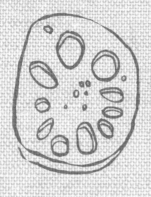

LOTUS FRUIT

CHILLIES

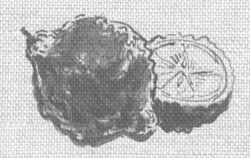

KAFFIR LIME

COURGETTE (ZUCCHINI)

CHINESE CABBAGE (PE-TSAÏ)

SHALLOT

MUSTARD

GARLIC

PAK CHOÏ

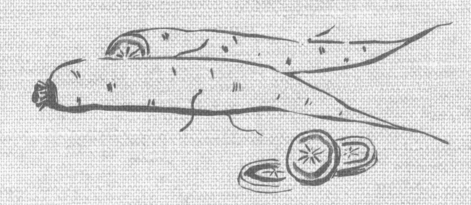

WHITE RADISH

AUBERGINE (EGGPLANT)

(BELL) PEPPERS

SHRIMP FRIED RICE

SERVES 4–6

Preparation: 25 min • **Cooking time:** 25 min

3 spring onions (scallions)

3 garlic cloves

2 limes

1 red (bell) pepper

10 Thai basil leaves

400g (14oz) prawns (shrimp)

2 tbsp groundnut (peanut) oil

600g (1lb 5oz/3½ cups) cooked rice

4 tbsp soy sauce

4 tbsp oyster sauce

1 pinch of chilli powder

Rinse, trim and chop the spring onions (scallions), peel and chop the garlic and squeeze the limes.

Trim the (bell) pepper, cut it open, deseed and remove the white membrane, then chop the flesh. Rinse and roughly chop the basil. Peel the prawns (shrimp).

Heat the oil in a large wok and fry the spring onions (scallions), garlic, (bell) pepper and prawns (shrimp) in the hot oil. Let them brown for 3–4 minutes, stirring constantly.

Next, add the rice and sauces. Reduce the heat a little and stir-fry for about 10 minutes until the rice becomes slightly crispy. Add the lime juice, chilli and basil, stir and cook for a further minute then turn off the heat and serve immediately.

THE RICE COOKER

White rice is to China what bread is to France, both a delicacy in its own right but also a basic accompaniment to any food or sauce. A meal without a bowl of rice is rare. It should be slightly sticky so that it is easy to pick up with chopsticks – a far cry from the famous non-stick rice sold in the West. A rice cooker is the best way to cook rice this way. Purchasing a rice cooker can be a real investment, in the same way that choosing and buying a computer can be. Some models, notably the Japanese ones, are very expensive, but they do allow you to cook perfect rice and keep it warm for 24 hours.

MISSO

Paris

Is Misso really a restaurant? Yes, in the Asian sense of the word. This restaurant offers only four place settings, but if you don't manage to get a seat, you can take away delicious Korean dishes prepared daily by the South Korean chef, who has lived in Paris for more than eight years. In the smallest of kitchens, she is able to produce vast quantities of a whole variety of typically Korean dishes. Halfway between Chinese and Japanese cuisine, Korean gastronomy is particularly fond of pickled products and fermented vegetables, including the famous *kimchi* (cabbage), which is prepared in many different ways: it can be more or less spicy, more or less fermented, or even white and washed. Misso's specialities are marinated beef, spiced pork with *kimchi*, Korean dumplings, chicken fritters and Korean pancakes, as well as the national dish, *bibimbap*, which is made with rice, vegetables, meat and eggs. The restaurant also caters for large orders as well as takeaways.

Opposite: At Misso's, the cook serves her speciality, *bibimbap*, in house and to take away.

STICKY RICE WITH CRISPY PORK BELLY

P. 332 • SERVES 4

Preparation: 20 min • **Soaking time:** 6 hr

Cooking time: 30 min

300g (10½oz/1½ cups) sticky rice, 1 garlic clove, 300g (10½oz) crispy pork belly, 5 tbsp soy sauce, 1 tsp caster (superfine)sugar, 2 tbsp white rice vinegar, 2 bunches of coriander (cilantro), 2 tbsp groundnut (peanut)oil

Rinse the rice – run water through it until it runs clear – then leave it to soak for 6 hours at room temperature. Peel and chop the garlic. Chop the pork into small pieces and put in a bowl with the soy sauce, garlic, sugar and rice vinegar. Marinate for 1 hour in the refrigerator. Rinse, dry and roughly chop the coriander (cilantro), including some of the stalks. Drain the rice then put it into a steaming basket and steam for 20 minutes. The cooked rice should be firm and slightly transparent. Heat the oil in a large wok and fry the pork and its marinade in the hot oil. Brown for a few minutes before adding the rice, stir and cook for 2 minutes. Add the coriander (cilantro) and serve.

FRAGRANT RICE WITH PORK

P. 333 • SERVES 6-8

Preparation: 20 min • **Marinating time:** 2 hr

Cooking time: 40 min

4 garlic cloves, 1 sweet onion, 500g (1lb 2oz) pork (shoulder or fillet, tenderloin), 2 tbsp caster (superfine) sugar, 2 tbsp white rice vinegar, 8 tbsp soy sauce, 2 green (bell) peppers, 400g (14oz/2 cups) fragrant rice, 1 tbsp turmeric, 1 tsp curry powder, 2 tbsp groundnut (peanut) oil

Peel and chop the garlic and onion. Cut the pork into small pieces then marinate it for 2 hours in the refrigerator with the sugar, rice vinegar, soy sauce, garlic and onion. Trim, deseed and chop the green (bell) peppers. Rinse the rice until the water runs clear. Put it into the rice cooker, cover with water to 1.5cm (⅝ inch) above the rice, add the turmeric and curry powder, stir and set to cook for 15 minutes. Alternatively cook the rice in a pan. Heat the oil in a large wok, add the (bell) peppers and cook for 1 minute then drain. Add the meat and marinade and cook for 6–7 minutes over a high heat. When the meat is cooked, add the rice and brown for 5 minutes, stirring. Add the peppers, mix and serve.

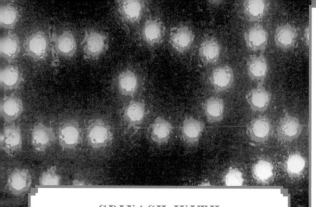

'BIBIMBAP' A KOREAN DISH OF RICE, BEEF AND VEGETABLES

P. 335 • SERVES 4

Preparation: 35 min • **Marinating time:** 45 min

Cooking time: 20 min

20g (¾oz) piece ginger, 2 carrots, 3 garlic cloves, 1 sweet onion, 1 courgette (zucchini), 400g (14oz) lean beefsteak (sirloin, rump, fillet, tenderloin), 4 tbsp Korean or Japanese soy sauce, 1 tbsp caster (superfine) sugar, 6 tbsp sesame oil, 100g (3½oz) green beans, 100g (3½oz/1 cup) bean sprouts, 20g (¾oz) spinach, 2 tsp roasted sesame seeds, 2 tbsp groundnut (peanut) oil, 150g (5½oz) bamboo shoots, 500g (1lb 2oz/scant 3 cups) cooked rice cooked, 4 eggs, 2 tbsp hot Korean sauce *(gochujang)*

Peel the ginger, carrots, garlic and onion. Grate the ginger and carrots and chop the garlic and onion. Trim and chop the courgette (zucchini). Cut the meat into thin slices and marinate for 45 minutes in the refrigerator with the soy sauce, sugar, 2 tbsp sesame oil, the garlic and ginger. Cook the vegetables separately in boiling salted water, allowing 5 minutes for the beans, 4 minutes for the courgette (zucchini) 2 minutes for the bean sprouts and 1 minute for the spinach. Season each vegetable with a little sesame oil and some sesame seeds. Heat 1 tbsp groundnut (peanut) oil in a pan, add the grated carrot and the bamboo shoots and cook for 2 minutes, then remove and keep warm. Heat the remaining 1 tbsp oil in the pan. Fry the onion for 2 minutes, then add the meat and its marinade and cook for 5 minutes. Divide the rice, vegetables and meat among four bowls. Fry the eggs then place on top. Sprinkle over sesame seeds and season with the sauce and the remaining sesame oil.

SPINACH WITH SESAME SAUCE

P. 334 • SERVES 4

Preparation: 25 min • Marinating **time:** 30 min

Cooking time: 20 min

50g (1¾oz) piece ginger, 1 tbsp chilli oil, 50ml (2fl oz/scant ¼ cup) hazelnut oil, 2 bunches of Chinese spinach (about 1.5kg/3lb), 1 tbsp soy sauce, 3 tbsp rice vinegar, 1 tsp caster (superfine) sugar, 150g (5½oz) tahini (sesame seed paste), 1 tsp roasted sesame seeds

Peel the ginger, then mix it in a bowl with the chilli oil and leave to stand for 10 minutes. Heat the hazelnut oil in a wok, add the ginger and stir-fry for 5 minutes until it is just crispy, then remove with a slotted spoon and set aside. Bring a pan of water to the boil and add the spinach (having rinsed it first and removed the stalks). Blanch for 2 minutes then drain and refresh in iced water. Squeeze out any remaining liquid, put on a plate and cover with the crispy ginger. Put the soy sauce, rice vinegar, sugar and 50ml (2fl oz/scant ¼ cup) cold water in a pan and leave until the sugar is fully dissolved. Add the tahini and bring to the boil, whisking it all the time, then leave to cool. When ready to serve, arrange the spinach in a dish and cover with the sauce. Leave to marinate for 30 minutes in a cool place, then sprinkle over the sesame seeds and serve.

FRIED AUBERGINE WITH PORK

SERVES 4

Preparation: 15 min • **Cooking time:** 20 min

30g (1oz) piece ginger
2 garlic cloves
1 bunch of spring onions (scallions)
3 nice ripe aubergines (eggplants)

3 tbsp groundnut (peanut) oil
150g (5½oz) minced (ground) pork (shoulder)
1 tsp chilli sauce
2 tbsp rice wine

1 tsp caster (superfine) sugar
4 tbsp soy sauce
2 tbsp white rice vinegar

Peel and grate the ginger, peel and crush the garlic and rinse and chop the spring onions (scallions). Rinse the aubergines (eggplants) then cut it into large pieces.

Heat the oil in a wok and fry the aubergine (eggplant) in the hot oil. Cook over a high heat for a few minutes until softened.

Add the minced (ground) pork, chilli sauce, ginger and garlic. Let it brown for a few moments then pour in the wine and 50ml (2fl oz/scant ¼ cup) water. Cook for 8–10 minutes until the cooking juices have evaporated.

Add the sugar, soy sauce and vinegar and cook over a high heat, stirring all the time, until caramelized. Add the spring onion (scallion), stir and turn off the heat. Serve with rice.

THE WOK

In Asian restaurants in the West, the vast majority of cooking is done in a wok, in which you can boil, fry or sear food quickly with very little fat. The ingredients keep their freshness and the vegetables stay crunchy. The wok has a rounded base, which enables a uniform and permanent contact between the ingredients and the heat source, thus cooking them homogeneously. Cooking in a wok requires constant attention. The woks sold in the West are adapted to our cookers and their bottom is flat, meaning that all the benefits of the shape are lost. Real woks do not have a non-stick coating: they are made of cast iron and it is the blackened residue that makes them non-stick, so they are rarely washed.

'KIMCHI' FERMENTED CABBAGE

P. 341 • SERVES 6

Preparation: 20 min • **Resting time:** 9 days

1 large Chinese cabbage, 180g (6½oz/scant 1 cup) salt, 3 garlic cloves, 100g (3½oz) piece ginger, 1 bunch of spring onions (scallions), 1 tbsp caster (superfine) sugar, 2 tbsp chilli powder

Cut the cabbage into four lengthways then in half again. Separate the leaves. Put a layer of cabbage in a large bowl, cover with salt, then add another layer, salt and continue until the cabbage and salt are finished. Place a plate with weights (a couple of cans will do) on top and leave to press for 5 days. Peel and chop the garlic. Peel and grate the ginger. Rinse and chop the spring onions (scallions), including the stems. Crush all these ingredients with the sugar and chilli in a mortar and pestle. Transfer the cabbage to a clean bowl, add the chilli paste and mix. Pack the cabbage into a plastic container with a lid, press to get rid of any air and leave to macerate for another 3 days at room temperature. Wrap the box in clingfilm (plastic wrap) to keep the air out. Stir and press down on the cabbage frequently to make sure the fermentation is regular and to get rid of any air. On the morning of the fourth day, put it in the refrigerator. The cabbage is ready to serve on day 5 accompanied with rice and grilled meat.

CRUNCHY GREEN BEANS WITH SESAME OIL

P. 342 • SERVES 4–6

Preparation: 20 min • **Cooking time:** 8 min

2 garlic cloves, 20g (¾oz) piece ginger, 1 small red chilli, 1 tbsp sesame oil, 1 pinch of Sichuan pepper, 5 tbsp soy sauce, 1 tsp rice vinegar, 1 tsp caster (superfine) sugar, 600g (1lb 5oz) green beans, salt, cooking oil

Peel and chop the garlic and ginger, then deseed the chilli and chop it finely. Heat the sesame oil in a pan. Add the garlic, ginger, chilli and Sichuan pepper and brown for 1 minute then add the soy sauce, vinegar and sugar. Turn off the heat and leave to cool. Trim the beans then rinse and dry them. Drop them into boiling salted water for 2 minutes, then drain, refresh and dry them. Prepare and heat a deep-fryer. Carefully lower the beans into the hot oil and deep-fry for about 5 minutes, shaking all the time. Drain onto a plate and serve with the spicy sesame oil.

'BAN CUON'

SERVES 4

Preparation: 30 min • **Resting time:** 45 min

Cooking time: 15 min

---

1 tbsp dried shrimps

20g (¾oz) black mushrooms

2 large onions

500g (1lb 2oz) pork

2 tbsp nuoc-mâm

(+ extra to serve)

4 tbsp groundnut (peanut) oil

a handful of bean sprouts

juice of 1 lemon

4 mint sprigs

4 coriander (cilantro) sprigs

2 tbsp fried shallots

For the pancake batter:

1 tea cup rice flour

1 tea cup cornflour (cornstarch)

3 tea cups water

2 tbsp groundnut (peanut) oil

a pinch of salt

Soak the shrimps in a bowl of water for 15 minutes until soft. Soak the black mushrooms in another bowl of warm water for 15 minutes to rehydrate them, then drain, rinse and remove any tough bits. Squeeze the mushrooms well and chop into pieces.

Peel and chop the onions, then chop the meat into small pieces. Mix the onion, meat, mushrooms and nuoc-mâm together in a bowl.

Heat 2 tbsp oil in a wok. Brown the meat and onions then add the shrimps and stir-fry for 10 minutes.

Now prepare the pancake batter. Whisk the rice flour and cornflour (cornstarch) with the water and oil and add the salt. The pancake batter should be quite liquid and smooth.

Cook the pancakes in a steamer for 10 minutes. To do this, spread a small amount of pancake mixture on a fine grill set over a pan of boiling water. Alternatively, use ready-made rice pancakes, which just need dampening first to soften them, then fill and warm in a steamer before serving.

Spread the pancakes out on a large sheet of oiled foil, divide the filling among the pancakes then fold up the sides to make little parcels. Keep them warm in a steamer over a pan of boiling water.

Fry the bean sprouts in a pan with the remaining oil. Serve the filled pancakes hot on a bed of fried bean sprouts. Cover with a sauce made of the nuoc-mâm, water and lemon juice and garnish with sprigs of coriander (cilantro), mint and fried shallots.

RECIPE PAGE 352

RECIPE
PAGE
352

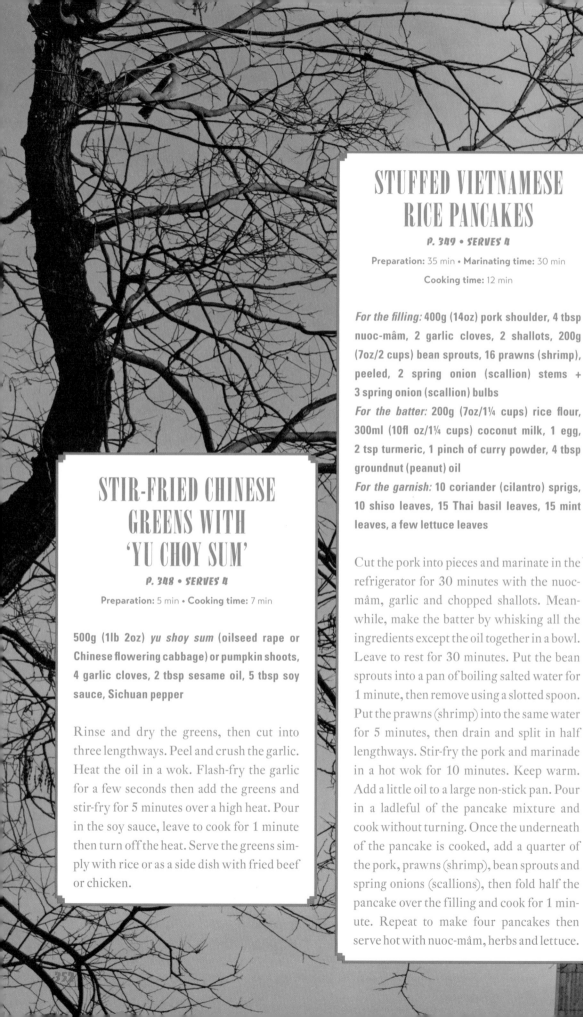

STUFFED VIETNAMESE RICE PANCAKES

P. 349 • *SERVES 4*

Preparation: 35 min • **Marinating time:** 30 min
Cooking time: 12 min

For the filling: 400g (14oz) pork shoulder, 4 tbsp nuoc-mâm, 2 garlic cloves, 2 shallots, 200g (7oz/2 cups) bean sprouts, 16 prawns (shrimp), peeled, 2 spring onion (scallion) stems + 3 spring onion (scallion) bulbs
For the batter: 200g (7oz/1¼ cups) rice flour, 300ml (10fl oz/1¼ cups) coconut milk, 1 egg, 2 tsp turmeric, 1 pinch of curry powder, 4 tbsp groundnut (peanut) oil
For the garnish: 10 coriander (cilantro) sprigs, 10 shiso leaves, 15 Thai basil leaves, 15 mint leaves, a few lettuce leaves

Cut the pork into pieces and marinate in the refrigerator for 30 minutes with the nuoc-mâm, garlic and chopped shallots. Meanwhile, make the batter by whisking all the ingredients except the oil together in a bowl. Leave to rest for 30 minutes. Put the bean sprouts into a pan of boiling salted water for 1 minute, then remove using a slotted spoon. Put the prawns (shrimp) into the same water for 5 minutes, then drain and split in half lengthways. Stir-fry the pork and marinade in a hot wok for 10 minutes. Keep warm. Add a little oil to a large non-stick pan. Pour in a ladleful of the pancake mixture and cook without turning. Once the underneath of the pancake is cooked, add a quarter of the pork, prawns (shrimp), bean sprouts and spring onions (scallions), then fold half the pancake over the filling and cook for 1 minute. Repeat to make four pancakes then serve hot with nuoc-mâm, herbs and lettuce.

STIR-FRIED CHINESE GREENS WITH 'YU CHOY SUM'

P. 348 • *SERVES 4*

Preparation: 5 min • **Cooking time:** 7 min

500g (1lb 2oz) *yu shoy sum* (oilseed rape or Chinese flowering cabbage) or pumpkin shoots, 4 garlic cloves, 2 tbsp sesame oil, 5 tbsp soy sauce, Sichuan pepper

Rinse and dry the greens, then cut into three lengthways. Peel and crush the garlic. Heat the oil in a wok. Flash-fry the garlic for a few seconds then add the greens and stir-fry for 5 minutes over a high heat. Pour in the soy sauce, leave to cook for 1 minute then turn off the heat. Serve the greens simply with rice or as a side dish with fried beef or chicken.

CANTONESE RICE

P. 351 SERVES 4

Preparation: 20 min • **Cooking time:** 25 min

1 sweet onion, 200g (7oz) crispy pork belly (see recipe p.336) or cooked ham or hock of ham, 4 tbsp groundnut (peanut) oil, 200g (7oz/2 cups) frozen peas, 2 eggs, 400g (14oz/2¼ cups) cooked fragrant rice

Peel and chop the onion, then chop the pork into small cubes and set aside. Heat the oil in a large wok. Sear the onion, pork and peas in the hot oil. Brown for 3–4 minutes then add the beaten eggs and cook for 5 minutes. Reduce the heat, use a spatula to break up the omelette then add the rice. Mix and stir-fry for 5–10 minutes. Serve piping hot as a main dish or as a side dish with fried beef or duck.

NOODLES

CHAO MIÀN
PAD. THAÏ
JIAOZI
NOUILLES SUIKAO
RÈ GÃN MIÀN
CHÀNGSHÒU MIÀN
LIANG PI
RAMEN
NAENGMYEON

NOODLES & OTHER VERMICELLI

Why is it that we talk about noodles for Chinese pasta and pasta for Italian noodles? Are noodles and pasta the same thing? On our plates perhaps, but in our heads definitely not. Noodles are functional food whereas pasta has a nobler character. Do Chinese noodles not merit the title of pasta? Flicking through the following pages and faced with their diversity of shapes and preparations, we can say without a doubt that Asian noodles are pasta like any other.

Pasta is said to have arrived from China at the time of Marco Polo but that's by no means certain. What is sure, however, is that the variety of Asian noodles, in terms of both types and recipes, puts Italy in the shade, despite the latter's renowned expertise in all things pasta.

Thick, thin, long or short, and made of wheat, buckwheat or rice, noodles and other Asian vermicelli are cooked in soup, but also fried, sautéed or grilled (broiled). In North China, people eat a lot of wheat noodles, while in the South, noodles are made with rice flour. In Thailand, *pad thai* is a dish of fried noodles with prawns (shrimp), egg, herbs and tofu. In Vietnam, noodles are served in soups and spring rolls, and nems are filled with vermicelli. Noodles are transparent, flat and quite thick, whereas vermicelli is very thin, light and white. In China, a show is made of pasta-making, when cooks stretch the dough to obtain long noodles (see p. 364). In recent years, noodles have become increasingly popular in the West and noodle restaurants have flourished throughout Europe and North America.

Noodles prepared by hand before being cooked and served with the soups.

Rice vermicelli.

A sign indicating that the restaurant serves congee, rice soup, at breakfast.

Wheat noodles of different widths, presented in a shop window.

359

2 carrots

1 leek

50g (¾oz) piece ginger

1.5kg (3lb) chuck beef or
stewing steak

2 marrow bones

3 star anise

1 bunch of spring onions
(scallions)

1 bunch of coriander (cilantro)

500g (1lb 2oz) fresh
rice noodles

Peel the carrots, rinse and dry the leek, then peel the ginger and chop it into fairly thick slices.

Tie the beef with string and put it into a casserole (Dutch oven) and cover with water to about 15cm (6 inches) above the level of the beef. Add the marrow bones, leek, carrots, ginger and star anise, bring to the boil then reduce the heat and simmer for 2 hours 30 minutes.

Rinse and chop the spring onions (scallions). Rinse and chop the coriander (cilantro), keeping part of the stalk. When the meat is cooked, drain it and cut it into thin slices. Strain the broth.

Drop the noodles into a pan of boiling salted water for a few minutes then drain and put them into four large bowls. Divide the slices of beef and the piping hot broth among the bowls. Sprinkle over the coriander (cilantro) and spring onion (scallion). Serve immediately.

LES PÂTES VIVANTES

Paris

At almost 60 years old, Xiaorong Coutin, a former radiologist of the Chinese army, is not afraid of hard work. Just as well, because producing her noodles twice a day requires a lot of energy. Her restaurant, which was opened during the mid-2000s in Paris's 9th *arrondissement*, immediately became an institution. People queue up at lunch time to taste her 'living pasta' which, we are told, is a family recipe. 'Their making requires so much courage and time that you only find them in families and not in restaurants in China.' Mrs Coutin is from Gansu, a province located in Northwestern China whose northern frontier borders Inner Mongolia. Here, where winters are harsh and summers sweltering, the noodles are eaten hot or cold, depending on the season. They are served with beef, pork or seafood, but also with lamb, a meat often eaten in this area. The restaurant has been so successful that a second one has opened in Paris and others should soon be appearing in Lyon and Lille.

Opposite: Mrs. Xiaorong Coutin pulls the noodles herself in front of clients and trains her restaurants' cooks.

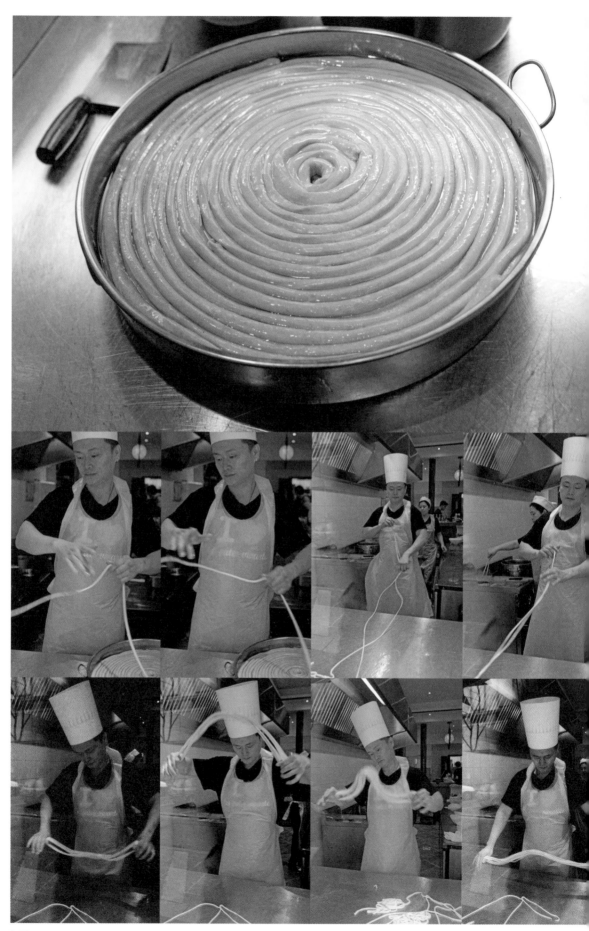

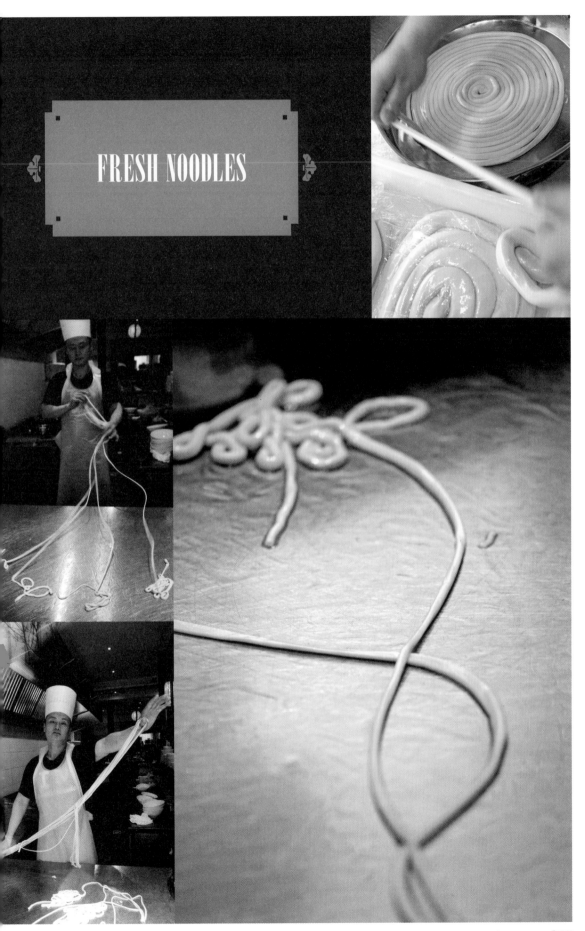

FRESH NOODLES

RECIPE
PAGE
370

'JIAOZI' PAN-FRIED CHINESE DUMPLINGS

P. 366 • SERVES 4–6

Preparation: 45 min • **Resting time:** 1 hr 30 min

Cooking time: 20 min

250g (9oz/2 cups) wheat flour, 30g (1oz) piece ginger, ½ bunch of spring onions (scallions), 2 garlic cloves, 500g (1lb 2oz) pork (half shoulder, half loin), 3 tbsp caster (superfine) sugar, 1 tbsp Chinese rice wine, 1 tbsp soy sauce, 2 tbsp groundnut (peanut) oil

Pour the flour into the bowl of a food mixer. Fix the hook attachment and knead slowly, adding the water a little at a time, until a smooth dough forms. If the dough sticks, add a little more flour. Wrap the dough in clingfilm (plastic wrap) and chill for 1 hour. Peel and chop the ginger. Rinse and chop the spring onions (scallions) and garlic. Put the meat through a mincer (grinder) with a fine grill, then mix the meat with the spring onion (scallion), ginger, garlic, and sugar. Add the wine and soy sauce. Knead the dough again and chill for another 30 minutes. Cut the dough in half, then divide each half into 20 balls. Flatten each ball of dough into a 10-cm (4-inch) disc and place a blob of filling at the centre of each one. Brush the edges of the dough with water, then fold them up over the filling and form little pleats to seal the dumpling. Heat the oil in a large pan over a high heat. Put the dumplings in the hot oil in a single layer and leave them to brown underneath without touching them. When fried, reduce the heat and pour in enough water to half cover them. Cover the pan with a lid and simmer until all the water has evaporated. Serve with a dipping sauce of soy sauce and vinegar.

NOODLE & VEGETABLE SALAD WITH SESAME

P. 367 • SERVES 4

Preparation: 35 min • **Cooking time:** 5 min

2 celery stalks, 200g (7oz) Swiss chard leaves, 100g (3½oz/⅔ cup) coarse salt, ½ a cucumber, 200g (7oz) large radish (pink, black or green), 4 garlic cloves, 3 tbsp sesame oil, 8 tbsp fermented black soy paste, 200g (7oz/2 cups) bean sprouts, 250g (9oz) dried noodles without egg, 150g (5½oz) can cooked mung beans

Rinse and chop the celery and Swiss chard leaves, then put them into two separate bowls and mix half the salt in to each. Leave for 30 minutes then rinse. Rinse, deseed and chop the cucumber without peeling it. Peel and grate the radish, then peel and chop the garlic. Heat the sesame oil in a wok. Sear the garlic in the hot oil until brown, then reduce the heat, add the soy paste, stir and leave to cool. Drop the bean sprouts into a pan of boiling salted water for 1 minute, then drain and refresh. Cook the noodles for a few minutes in a large pan of boiling salted water then drain and refresh for 1 minute in ice-cold water. Arrange the cold noodles in four large bowls. Divide the vegetables and the beans over the noodles. Put the soy paste into four ramekin dishes and serve, mixing the noodles, vegetables and the soy paste in each bowl.

FRIED NOODLES WITH VEGETABLES

P. 367 • SERVES 4–6

Preparation: 25 min • **Cooking time:** 20 min

1 bunch of spring onions (scallions), 1 sweet onion, 2 garlic cloves, 50g (1¾oz) piece ginger, 2 carrots, 2 Chinese cabbage leaves, 1 red (bell) pepper, 150g (5½oz/1½ cups) bean sprouts, 600g (1lb 5oz) fresh egg noodles, 3 tbsp groundnut (peanut) oil, 4 tbsp soy sauce, 3 tbsp oyster sauce

Rinse and chop the spring onions (scallions). Peel the sweet onion, garlic, ginger and carrots. Finely chop the onion and garlic, grate the ginger and carrots. Rinse and chop the cabbage leaves. Trim, deseed and chop the (bell) pepper. Drop the bean sprouts into boiling water for 1 minute then drain them. Cook the noodles for 5 minutes in boiling water. They should remain firm. Drain. Heat the oil in a large wok. Fry the onion and garlic in the hot oil for 1 minute until brown then add the bean sprouts, carrots, cabbage, pepper and ginger and cook for 2 minutes before adding the noodles, soy sauce and oyster sauce. Add the spring onion (scallion), stir and cook for 3 minutes over a high heat. Serve.

'PAD THAI'

P. 368 • SERVES 4

Preparation: 20 min • **Soaking time:** 20 min

Cooking time: 10 min

200g (7oz) dried rice tagliatelle, 150g (5½oz/1½ cups) bean sprouts, 2 garlic cloves, 2 spring onions (scallions), 150g (5½oz) prawns (shrimp), ½ a bunch of Chinese chives , 50g (1¾oz/⅓ cup) roasted peanuts, 2 tbsp groundnut (peanut) oil, 1 tsp cane sugar, 2 tbsp nuoc-mâm, 2 tbsp oyster sauce, 1 tsp chilli powder, juice of 1 lime

Soak the rice tagliatelle in warm water for 20 minutes. Drop the bean sprouts into a pan of boiling water for 1 minute, drain and set aside. Peel and chop the garlic, then trim and chop the spring onions (scallions) with their stems. Peel the prawns (shrimp), snip the chives with scissors and crush the peanuts in a mortar and pestle. Drain the tagliatelle and set aside. Heat the oil in a large wok. Fry the garlic, prawns (shrimp) and spring onions (scallions) in the hot oil until brown. Add the tagliatelle, bean sprouts, sugar, nuoc-mâm, oyster sauce and chilli and stir-fry for 5–6 minutes. Add the chives, lime juice and peanuts, mix together and serve.

FRIED NOODLES WITH SEAFOOD

P. 372 • SERVES 4

Preparation: 25 min • **Cooking time:** 20 min

2 garlic cloves, 1 bunch of spring onions (scallions), 200g (7oz) squid (not the tentacles), 250g (9oz) prawns (shrimp), 200g (7oz) scallops, 400g (14oz) fresh fat egg noodles, 2 tbsp groundnut (peanut) oil, 2 leaves of Chinese cabbage, 4 tbsp soy sauce

Peel and chop the garlic and rinse and chop the spring onions (scallions). Cut the squid into small squares then make little cuts into the flesh to help tenderize it on cooking. Peel the prawns (shrimp) and cut the scallops in half. Cook the noodles briefly in boiling water, then drain and refresh for 1 minute in ice-cold water. Heat the oil in a large wok. Fry the garlic and the chopped cabbage leaves in the hot oil. Brown for a few seconds then add the seafood. Cook everything over a high heat. Add the noodles, spring onions (scallions) and soy sauce. Mix and cook for 3 minutes then arrange the noodles on plates. Serve immediately.

PAN-FRIED CHINESE DUMPLINGS WITH PRAWNS

P. 373 • SERVES 4

Preparation: 45 min • **Resting time:** 30 min

Cooking time: 5 min

1 bunch of spring onions (scallions), 200g (7oz) prawns (shrimp), 100g (3½oz) minced (ground) pork, 1 egg (separated), 1 tbsp nuoc-mâm, 20 small wonton pastry squares, cooking oil
For the sauce: 2 tbsp nuoc-mâm, 1½ tbsp rice vinegar, 1½ tbsp warm water, 20g (¾oz/5 tsp) caster (superfine) sugar, juice of 1 lime, 1 small red chilli, chopped (optional)

Rinse and chop the spring onions (scallions). Peel the prawns (shrimp) and chop in a food mixer then mix with the pork, egg white, nuoc-mâm and spring onions (scallions). Baste the wonton squares with the egg yolk mixed with a little water. Put a small amount of filling on each square, fold up the dough over the filling and, using your fingers, press down firmly to seal. Leave to rest for 30 minutes. Prepare and heat a deep-fryer. Drop the dumplings into the hot oil five at a time. Leave them to turn golden for 4–5 minutes moving all the time with a slotted spoon, then drain on kitchen paper (paper towels). Serve piping hot with the sauce.

EGG NOODLES WITH SPRING ONIONS

P. 375 SERVES 6

Preparation: 20 min • **Cooking time:** 20 min

2 garlic cloves, 1 bunch of spring onions (scallions), 500g (1lb 2oz) fresh egg noodles, 1 tbsp groundnut (peanut) oil, 50ml (2fl oz/scant ¼cup) chicken stock, 2 tbsp soy sauce

Peel and chop the garlic. Wash and finely chop the spring onions (scallions). Drop the noodles into a large pan of boiling water for 5 minutes then drain them. They should remain slightly firm. Heat the oil in a large wok. Fry the garlic in the hot oil then add the chicken stock and the soy sauce. Let it reduce by half before adding the noodles and spring onion. Cook for 3 minutes, stirring all the time. Serve nice and hot.

TEAS
DRINKS
DESSERT

茶

You wouldn't dream of drinking tea around a table in Asia, and as for eating sweet dishes at the end of the meal, well, Asian traditions don't stretch that far. We need to change our way of doing things. Flambéed banana fritters are a Western invention; Chinese nougat as a dessert at the end of a meal is rare in its country of origin; and as for ice cream and sponge cake, which is often offered as a dessert in Chinese restaurants, that too is Western. If you want to enjoy authentic sweet flavours, you will probably have to do so during the meal itself and agree to eat/drink a mixture of coconut milk, water chestnuts, fluorescent jelly and red and/or white beans. But it makes a change from apple tart!

TEA & OTHER BEVERAGES

Tea is the most consumed drink in the world, after pure water and China is the largest consumer of tea in terms of the quantity of the liquid drunk. However, if we take into account the weight of the tea leaves used, the Chinese are far behind the Irish, the English and even the Russians, the reason being that the Chinese infuse the same tea leaves five, ten or even fifteen times. Asians do not drink while eating, but rather after they have eaten, except for dim sum meals. All of the Southeast Asian (Vietnam, Cambodia, Laos) and Northeast Asian (Japan, Korea) countries produce tea, but it is China that is the true home of tea, and the best teas in the world are found in continental China and on the island of Taiwan. In the West, it is common to drink tea – whether hot tea or iced tea, green tea, or even a scented tea – while eating in Asian restaurants, which would be inconceivable in Asian countries. A new fashion from

Taiwan has recently arrived in the West: bubble tea. This is a slightly fruity green or black tea, plain or with milk, served in a glass at the bottom of which swim large balls of tapioca that you have to suck up with an extra-large straw.

Tea is not, however, the only beverage consumed in Asia: Asian beer is also frequently drunk. Chinese, Thai, Cambodian and Vietnamese beers are very light and are served well chilled. Soft drinks are also complementary to spicy food, but whatever your beverage, it should be drunk chilled and from the bottle. In countries where good wines are readily available, white wines such as Chardonnay, gewürztraminer or Sauvignon Blanc are often recommended to accompany the fragrant Thai cuisine, and at the end of the meal, some Chinese restaurants in the West offer guests warm or chilled rice wine served in small porcelain cups or glasses.

Banana fritters and candied fruit for sale
in Montreal's Chinatown

Street scene in New York

Take away Jian Dui

Multicoloured prawn (shrimp) crackers for sale in
the new Chinatown in Brooklyn

Fermented rice beverage.

Dessert consisting of small fritters, ginger syrup and coconut pulp (Bangkok)

COCONUT BALLS

P. 388. MAKES 10 BALLS

Preparation: 40 min • **Soaking time:** overnight

Cooking time: 1 hr 20 min

50g (1¾oz/scant ¼ cup) yellow mung beans, 250g (9oz/1¾ cups) glutinous rice flour, 50g (1¾oz/¼ cup) caster (superfine) sugar, 200ml (7fl oz/generous ¾ cup) warm water, 30g (1oz/ ¼ cup) icing (confectioners') sugar, 40g (1½oz/ ½ cup) grated coconut + 100g (3½oz/generous 1 cup), to decorate

Soak the beans in water overnight. The next day, drain and put them into a pan and cover with water 5cm (2 inches) above their level. Bring to the boil then simmer for 1 hour over a low heat. Mix the flour in a bowl with the sugar and water and knead by hand until it is a soft, pliable dough. Drain the beans then mix them with the icing (confectioners') sugar and coconut. Cool, then form into small balls 1.5cm (⅝ inch) in diameter. Divide the dough into small pieces (10g/¼oz each), roll into balls and flatten to make discs. Wrap each ball of the filling in a disc of dough and roll together to make balls. Steam for 20 minutes then roll in grated coconut while still hot. Serve the same day, reheated in the microwave.

BUBBLE TEA

P. 389 • SERVES 4

Preparation: 15 min

200ml (7fl oz/ generous ¾ cup) black tea, 200ml (7fl oz/generous ¾ cup) milk, 100ml (3½fl oz/ scant ½ cup) coconut milk, 1 tbsp cane sugar, a few ice cubes, 150g (5½oz) cooked pearl tapioca, 80g (3oz) red beans or sweet red bean paste, 4 tbsp mint syrup, 4 tbsp strawberry syrup, 8 tbsp mango or peach coulis

Mix the tea with the milk, coconut milk and cane sugar in a shaker. Add a few ice cubes and shake well. Share the tapioca and beans out into large glasses. Pour in the milky coconut tea and add the mint and raspberry syrups and coulis to taste. Serve with ice cubes and a large straw.

TOFFEE APPLES

P. 390 • SERVES 4

Preparation: 10 min • **Cooking time:** 10 min

8 very small red apples, 50ml (2fl oz/scant ¼ cup) water, 250g (9oz) sugar cubes, 30g (1oz) glucose, a little red food colouring

Rinse and dry the apples. Put the water, sugar, glucose and food colouring in a pan, bring to the boil, then reduce the heat and simmer without stirring until it is a pale caramel. Turn off the heat and cool for 2 minutes. Stick a wooden skewer into each apple then lower them one at a time into the pan to coat them with a layer of caramel. Place the coated apples on a wire rack and leave them to cool before serving.

CHINESE NOUGAT

P. 391 • MAKES 300G (11OZ)

Preparation: 30 min • **Cooking time:** 20 min

Setting time: 3 hr

70g (2½oz/½ cup) whole peanuts, 145g (5oz) sugar cubes, 300ml (10fl oz/1¼ cups) water, 20g (¾oz/2½ tbsp) manioc flour, ½ tsp agar-agar 1 heaped tsp roasted sesame seeds

Shell the peanuts, remove the skins and toss them in a dry frying pan to colour them slightly. Put the sugar cubes in a pan and cook over a low heat, stirring constantly with a wooden spoon, until you have a light caramel. Stir in half the water, keeping the pan over a low heat, until the caramel is soft. Whisk the rest of the water with the manioc flour in a bowl. Pour in the caramel, add the agar-agar and mix. Toss the peanuts in the pan the caramel was in for 3 minutes then pour in the contents of the bowl. Add half the sesame seeds. Heat and stir with a wooden spoon until it is a golden syrup then pour the nougat into an oiled baking dish. Leave the nougat to set for 3 hours. Turn the nougat out and chop it into thick squares, then roll the squares in the remaining sesame seeds and serve.

Puer cake, a tea that
can be stored like a
great vintage wine

Sale of tea by weight

Engraving on a mug used to drink tea

Flavoured iced tea (Singapore)

Tea tasting.

Thermos of hot water, a
ubiquitous object in everyday
family life

Tea is vacuum-packed for easy transportation

TEA CEREMONY

DEEP-FRIED SESAME-SEED BALLS

MAKES 15 BALLS

Preparation: 45 min • **Cooking time:** 45 min • **Resting time:** 2 hr 20 min

For the dough:
1 small potato
(a starchy variety)
120g (4oz/scant 1 cup)
glutinous rice flour
30g (1oz/scant ¼ cup)
rice flour
30g (1oz/¼ cup) wheat flour

60g (2oz/½ cup) icing
(confectioners') sugar
1 sachet of yeast
a pinch of salt
130ml (4½fl oz/½ cup)
warm water
100g (3½oz) light sesame seeds
cooking oil

For the filling:
125g (4½oz) yellow mung beans
75g (2½oz/⅔ cup) icing
(confectioners') sugar
1 x 11g (¼ oz) packet vanilla
sugar

Leave the beans to soak overnight in a bowl of water.

The next day, preheat the oven to 200°C/400°F/Gas Mark 6 then bake the unpeeled potato for 35 minutes. Remove the skin, mash the cooked flesh with a fork and pass it through a sieve.

Drain the beans, put them into a saucepan and pour in enough water to cover them by 5cm (2 inches). Bring to the boil, reduce the heat and leave to simmer for 1 hour.

Make the dough. Mix the flours in a bowl with the icing (confectioners') sugar, yeast, salt, potato flesh and warm water. Knead into a soft dough with your hands, then wrap in clingfilm (plastic wrap) and chill in the refrigerator for 2 hours.

To make the filling, drain the beans and mix them with the icing (confectioners') sugar and vanilla sugar. Leave to chill.

Roll the chilled filling into 1.5-cm (⅝-inch) balls, adding a little water if it is too crumbly. Roll the dough in your hands to make ping-pong sized balls. Flatten them slightly with your fingers. Put a ball of filling in the centre of each one then fold up the sides and roll again to form large smooth balls. Roll in the sesame seeds, pressing them in gently, then chill for 20 minutes.

Prepare and heat a deep-fryer to 140°C/284°F. Carefully lower the balls into the hot oil three at a time and deep-fry for 10–12 minutes. Drain on kitchen paper (paper towels) and leave to cool before serving.

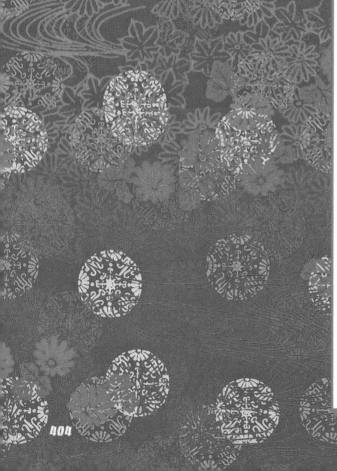

CHILLED JASMINE TEA WITH LEMONGRASS

P. 401 • SERVES 4

Preparation: 15 min

4 lemongrass stalks, 1 litre (1¾ pints/4 cups) water, 3 jasmine tea bags, 2 tbsp cane sugar, 30 ice cubes

Roughly chop the lemongrass. Boil the water then drop in the tea bags and let them infuse for a few minutes. Pour into a large jug (pitcher), add the sugar and lemongrass, stir and leave to infuse until completely cool. Strain the tea into large glasses and add the ice cubes. Leave to chill in the refrigerator for 5 minutes and serve.

LEMONADE

P. 402 • SERVES 4

Preparation: 10 min • **Resting time:** 2 hr

10 small limes, 200g (7oz/1 cup) caster (superfine) sugar, 1.5 litres (2½ pints/6⅓ cups) mineral water, 1 tube of yellow food colouring, ice cubes

Squeeze the limes. Mix the sugar and the water together in a jug (pitcher) then stir until the sugar dissolves. Add the lime juice, then the colouring. Stir and strain into a jug (pitcher). Chill for 2 hours before serving with ice cubes.

CANDIED GINGER

P. 403 • SERVES 4

Soaking time: 5 hr

Preparation: 10 min • **Resting time:** overnight

Cooking time: 30 min • **Drying time:** 24 hr

300g (10½oz) piece ginger, 300g (10½oz/1½ cups) caster (superfine) sugar (+ extra for sprinkling)

Soak the ginger in water for 5 hours. Peel and chop it then rinse it 2 or 3 times. Cook the ginger for 3 minutes in a pan of boiling water. When it is cooked (check by sticking in the tip of a knife), rinse, drain, then spread out on a clean cloth and leave to dry overnight. The next day, put the ginger in a pan with 1 tsp water and the sugar. Let it cook very slowly until the liquid has evaporated. Drain the ginger carefully, taking care to coat each slice with the melted sugar. Spread out the slices on a sheet of greaseproof (wax) paper. Sprinkle with caster (superfine) sugar and leave to dry for 24 hours before serving.

紹興花彫酒

SHAO HSING HUA TIAO CHIEW

RECIPE INDEX

STARTERS

'Goi cuon' spring rolls	P. 18
Vietnamese prawn salad	P. 20
Shrimp and pork rolls	P. 26
Spring rolls with crab and pork	P. 26
Saigon crab nems	P. 27
'Amok'	P. 27
'Yam' with beef	P. 28
Crispy prawns with tamarind sauce	P. 32
'Nems' spring rolls	P. 34

CHINESE DUMPLINGS

'Baozi' stuffed buns	P. 44
'Ha Kao' prawn dumplings	P. 46
Juicy pork dumplings	P. 54
Prawn and spinach dumplings	P. 55

SOUPS & BROTHS

Pekinese soup	P. 70
Fish broth with fish dumplings	P. 72
'Kway teow' soup with pork and prawn	P. 78
Broth with wonton dumplings	P. 79
Chinese fondue	P. 79
Chicken soup with noodles	P. 80
Crab and asparagus soup	P. 82
Thai chicken soup with coconut milk	
'Tom kha kaï'	P. 88
'Hu tieu' soup with quail's eggs	P. 88
Sweet-and-sour Chinese soup	P. 89
Pho soup	P. 98

CHICKEN & QUAIL

Chicken and rice	P. 110
General Tao's chicken	P. 118
Sweet-and-sour chicken with pineapple	P. 119
Stuffed chicken wings with vermicelli and mushrooms	P. 119
Quail with five spice	P. 122
Chicken curry with aubergine	P. 124
Caramelized chicken with sesame	P. 130
Fried chicken balls with basil and chilli	P. 131
Fried chicken with cashew nuts	P. 131

BEEF

Fried beef with basil	P. 142
Fried beef with curry	P. 148
'Lot lac'	P. 149
'Bo bun'	P. 149
Raw beef Thai style	P. 158
Fried beef with pepper and satay sauce	P. 159
'Bun Bo Lui' bun cha beef	P. 159
Fried beef with onions	P. 160
Fried beef with broccoli	P. 162

PORK

Cantonese pork spare ribs	P. 174
Sweet-and-sour pork with basil	P. 176
Grilled pork chops with lemongrass	P. 182
Caramelized pork	P. 182
Hanoi 'bun cha'	P. 183
Pork belly with chestnuts	P. 184
Soup with glazed pork, noodles and dumplings	P. 186
'Nem nuong' grilled pork balls	P. 196
'Tonkatsu'	P. 197
Shredded pork with bamboo shoots	P. 197

Previous pages: Procession of the lions, a symbol of prosperity during Chinese New Year celebrations

DUCK

Glazed Peking duck to make at home	P. 214
Pancakes	P. 215
Fried duck with pineapple	P. 222
Fried duck with bamboo shoots	P. 230
Duck rice	P. 230
Fried duck with vegetables and crispy noodles	P. 231
Five-spice roast duck	P. 232
Fried duck with fresh pepper and basil	P. 238
Roast duck soup with egg noodles	P. 238
Cheat's Peking duck with hoisin sauce	P. 239

FISH & SEAFOOD

Fried shrimp with hot sauce	P. 252
Chinese steamed fish	P. 258
Steamed Shanghai hairy crabs	P. 258
Steamed crabs with Vietnamese sauce and kumquats	P. 259
Chilli crab	P. 259
Fried squid with spring onion	P. 260
Deep-fried fish with garlic and chilli sauce	P. 262
Stuffed crab with pork and rice noodles	P. 268
Fried fish with sweet-and-sour sauce	P. 268
Deep-fried prawns	P. 269
'Chao tom'	P. 269
Fried fish with broth and coriander	P. 270
Salt and pepper prawns	P. 272
Fried prawns with pineapple	P. 274

WEIRD & WONDERFUL

Slow-cooked sea cucumber with pumpkin	P. 294
Chicken feet	P. 296
Curried fish head	P. 302
Steamed tentacles with soy sauce	P. 302
Frogs' legs with coconut milk and basil	P. 302
Jellyfish salad with chicken	P. 303
Traditional shark's fin soup	P. 306
Tofu with 100-year-old eggs	P. 308
Slow-cooked abalones with asparagus	P. 312

VEGETABLES, RICE & SIDE DISHES

Shrimp fried rice	P. 328
Sticky rice with crispy pork belly	P. 336
Fragrant rice with pork	P. 336
Spinach with sesame sauce	P. 337
'Bibimbap': a Korean dish of rice, beef and vegetables	P. 337
Fried aubergine with pork	P. 338
'Kimchi' fermented cabbage	P. 344
Crunchy green beans with sesame oil	P. 345
'Ban cuon'	P. 346
Stir-fried Chinese greens with 'yu choy sum'	P. 352
Stuffed Vietnamese rice pancakes	P. 352
Cantonese rice	P. 353

NOODLES

Fresh noodles with beef and coriander	P. 360
Pan-fried Chinese dumplings 'Jiaozi'	P. 370
Noodle and vegetable salad with sesame	P. 370
'Pad thai'	P. 371
Fried noodles with vegetables	P. 371
Fried noodles with seafood	P. 376
Pan-fried Chinese dumplings with prawns	P. 376
Egg noodles with spring onions	P. 377

TEA, DRINKS & DESSERT

Coconut balls	P. 392
Bubble tea	P. 392
Toffee apples	P. 392
Chinese nougat	P. 393
Deep-fried sesame-seed balls	P. 398
Chilled jasmine tea with lemongrass	P. 404
Lemonade	P. 404
Candied ginger	P. 404

CHINATOWNS AROUND THE WORLD

Chinatowns exist in nearly every major city around the world and life within them often resembles life in China. The residents speak both Cantonese or Mandarin and their new country's language and the street signs are usually in both languages, but every Chinatown is different. Some are just a couple of streets long while others are much larger; but whatever their size, they are a major feature in the cities where they are located.

Covering more than five square kilometres (two square miles), the Chinatown in Manhattan, New York is the largest in North America. It also has the largest population of Chinese immigrants in the West.

San Francisco's Chinatown is the largest on the West Coast and is the oldest in the US. It was established in the 1840s when Chinese people came looking for gold in the gold-rush days. After it was destroyed in the 1906 earthquake, US architects were instructed to rebuild it to make it look more Chinese than the original. It covers 24 square blocks and consists of various alleys and streets. Chicago also has a Chinatown, which was established in 1905 and is the second oldest settlement in the United States.

Chinatown in Vancouver is Canada's largest Chinatown and the third largest in the North America. It is located on the eastern side of downtown Vancouver and was established in the 1890s when early Chinese immigrants arrived to work on the railways and in the mines. It became a booming business district and home to lots of restaurants, temples and markets.

The Chinatown in London has been located in a variety of places. It was first established in the 1800s in the East End when Chinese sailors settled there, but it moved after it was bombed in the Blitz and there was a global decline in shipping. The present Chinatown is in Soho and is a major tourist attraction as well as an important cultural focal point for the Chinese community. The Chinatown in Liverpool, located in the heart of the city, is the oldest in Europe and dates back to the late 1850s when a direct shipping service was set up between Britain and China. It also boasts the largest arch located at the gateway to a Chinatown outside China. Manchester's Chinatown is the second largest in the UK and the third largest in Europe. It was first established in the early twentieth century when Chinese restaurants opened up, so its roots were in business.

There are Chinatowns in most major European cities including Antwerp, Amsterdam, Berlin (where there are two) and Paris, as well as in Italy, Poland, Russia, Spain and Portugal.

The Chinatown in Melbourne was established in the 1850s when Chinese immigrants travelled to Australia in search of gold. It is the longest continuous Chinese settlement in the West and is an important economic and social hub for the Chinese community there.

Sydney's Chinatown is the largest in Australia and is currently located in the southern part of the central business district, where is was established in the 1920s. It boasts some of the best food outside Asia.

ADDRESSES

Les Pâtes Vivantes
46, rue du Faubourg-Montmartre, 75009 Paris, +33 1 45 23 10 21
3, rue de Turbigo, 75001 Paris, +33 1 40 13 08 04
www.lespatesvivantes.net

Au délice de Confucius
68, boulevard de l'Hôpital, 75013 Paris, +33 1 45 87 23 37, www.deliceshandong.com

Chez Vong
10, rue de la Grande-Truanderie, 75001 Paris, +33 1 40 39 99 89,
www.chez-vong.com

Dong Huong
14, rue Louis-Bonnet, 75011 Paris, +33 1 43 57 39 90,
www.dong-huong.com

Pho 99
119, allée du Parc-de-Choisy, 75013 Paris, +33 1 45 83 00 12

Misso
27, rue du Moulin-des-Prés, 75013 Paris, +33 1 53 62 15 72

Sukho thai
12, rue du Père-Guérin, 75013 Paris, +33 1 45 81 55 88

Bo Ky
80, Bayard Street, Manhattan, New York +1 212 406 22 92
www.bokynyc.com

456 Shanghai Cuisine
69, Mott Sreet, Manhattan, New York, +1 212 964 0003
www.456shanghaicuisine.co

ACKNOWLEDGEMENTS

I wish to thank Catherine Saunier-Talec, Anne La Fay, Valérie Ballot and Antoine Béon, who believed in this project and who trusted me during its making. I thank Lisa Grall for the efficiency in managing this project.

Thank you to all the people I met in New York, Paris, Montreal, Hong Kong, Singapore, Bangkok and Beijing for having given me access to the kitchens of their restaurants and allowing me to take pictures and use recipes in this book.

Thank you to Tamara Lui.

Thank you to Marie-Paule Jaulme and Emanuelle Jary, my faithful collaborators, for their patience and their huge investment in this project.

First published in the UK, USA and Australia in 2015 by:

Jacqui Small LLP
74–77 White Lion Street
London N1 9PF

First published by Hachette Livre, Paris, 2014

© Hachette Livre (Hachette Pratique), 2014

ISBN: 9781910254233

Publisher: Jacqui Small
Translator: Kate Rignell
Editor: Kathy Steer
Art Direction: Antoine Beon
Design: Marie-Paul Jaulme

Printed in China